Women Studying Childcare
Integrating lives through adult education

Women Studying Childcare
Integrating lives through adult education

Hazel R Wright

Anglia Ruskin University

Trentham Books

Stoke on Trent, UK and Sterling, USA

Trentham Books Limited
Westview House   22883 Quicksilver Drive
734 London Road   Sterling
Oakhill   VA 20166-2012
Stoke on Trent   USA
Staffordshire
England ST4 5NP

First published 2011

British Library Cataloguing-in-Publication Data
A catalogue record for this book is available from the
British Library

ISBN 978 1 85856 485 2

Designed and typeset by Trentham Books Ltd
Printed and bound in Great Britain by 4edge Limited, Hockley

Contents

Chapter 7
Considering the consequences of studying • 113
Individual gains
Social gains
Effects on family
Vocational adjustments
Stepping up
Inching forward
Seeking better conditions in schools
Focusing frustration
Educational impacts
Residual learning
Learning processes
Further study
Too much too soon
Integrated lives

Chapter 8
Meeting women's needs: heeding women's strengths • 133
Revisiting the strands
Reviewing the links
Considering gender
Extending integrated lives theory
Transition and growth
Living in a slowly shifting present
Conceptualising instability
Living at the micro-level
Considering policy implications

Acronyms

BAECE	British Association for Early Childhood Education
CA	Capability Approach
CACE	Central Advisory Council for Education
CRB	Criminal Records Bureau
CWDC	Children's Workforce Development Council
DCSF	Department for Children, Schools and Families
DES	Department of Education and Science
DfE	Department for Education
DfEE	Department for Education and Employment
DfES	Department for Education and Skills
DoH	Department of Health
EYPS	Early Years Professional Status
FdA	Foundation Degree
FE	Further Education
(G)C(S)E	(General) Certificate of (Secondary) Education
HE	Higher Education
HMSO	Her Majesty's Stationery Office
IEP	Individual Education Plan
NFER	National Foundation for Educational Research
NIACE	National Institute for Adult and Continuing Education
NVQ	National Vocational Qualification

Ofsted	Office for Standards in Education
PhD	Doctor of Philosophy
PVI	Private, voluntary, independent (sector)
QCA	Qualification and Curriculum Agency
SCAA	School Curriculum and Assessment Authority
SRHE	Society for Research into Higher Education
TA	Teaching Assistant
UK	United Kingdom
UN	United Nations
UNESCO	United Nations Educational, Scientific and Cultural Organisation

Preface

As its title implies, this book describes and analyses the stories of a group of mature women who decided to train as childcare workers. It stems from a qualitative study that focused on the role of education in their lives. Thus, it makes informed comments on aspects of the early years sector in England but does not pretend to be a balanced or exhaustive study of the profession and should not be viewed as such. The study followed an open and emergent design that left the students to determine what they talked about. It found that education was only one aspect of their narratives, for their main concern was to integrate the many different elements in their lives. Thus their accounts of family, of work, of friendship and community relationships are as important as their educational experiences and all play a role in explaining the choices they make.

As a social scientist with an early years specialism, I approached both the research and this book from a multidisciplinary standpoint. I was keen to engage with an early years audience but also to develop broader perspectives as I believe it to be important that those of us who work in the field of childcare continually strive to deepen our understanding of the society in which we live. Thus, the book introduces theory from sociology, psychology and economics and refers to wider educational and historical contexts when relevant. In so doing, it hopes to appeal to researchers, adult educators, sociologists and other social scientists – particularly those interested in gender studies – in addition to a core audience of early years workers. Some of you may, like me, have an interest in all these fields. Others may relate to a particular discipline, even to a single strand within the childcare workforce. The book strives to explain terms clearly, and offers fuller definitions in the concept catalogue, to maximise accessibility.

To help you hear the data speak for itself, I should explain a number of conventions. As part of the process of clarifying meaning in the original analysis, I coded complex sections of text to show the structures in the speech. This, however, reduces readability so the codes do not appear in this book except in two circumstances. I use ellipses ... to indicate that text has been omitted from quoted material, usually to excise excess words and repetition. When the ellipses are bracketed (...) this indicates that the speaker paused or omitted key words, often assuming an understanding on the part of the listener. Additionally, (cc) indicates that a term appears in the concept catalogue. The student names are all fictitious and, actually, replacements for numeric codes that were used during the research process. They are thus doubly distanced from the real names of the research participants and this should assist anonymity. I have tried to avoid substituting names that could refer to students I have regularly taught elsewhere but inevitably there will be some overlaps given the timescales and numbers involved.

Finally, I should explain that my choice of childcare, as a label in this work, stems from a belief that its simplicity and familiarity establishes an appropriate tone within a narrative account. The term is more concise than phrases like early years education or early childhood education and less hard-edged than acronyms like EYE, ECEC, and ECCE, and in its contemporary usage is deemed to embrace both educational and care aspects.

Acknowledgements

I owe thanks to a considerable number of people who indirectly contributed to the writing of this book, in particular the students who agreed to take part in the research. My friends and family provided encouragement and practical help when needed and my work places, both college and university, allowed a degree of flexible working to enable me to carry out the project.

For academic support during the research process, I thank Tom Ling, David Skinner, Janet Nicholls and Alan Wilson; and for commenting on the final manuscript from an early years perspective, colleagues Gillian Gresham and Paulette Luff. Their combined suggestions considerably improved the coherence and clarity of this work but any errors or omissions are mine alone.

I am grateful to Gillian Klein and the staff at Trentham Books for taking a risk on a little known author and supporting this publication to fruition. I hope that you, the reader, will buy your own copy of this book so that they make some return on their investment in me – I am told that the book is quite interesting!

1

Introducing the research project

In telling the *real* stories of women studying childcare, this book adds a human element to the growing discourse around professionalism and standards. It draws upon research designed to look at the value of adult education in a childcare context but found that there is a much broader picture to paint: that of women living complex integrated lives and continually striving to balance the competing demands of family, friends and community without losing sight of their own needs and desires. This is a picture that emerges from a long historical tradition in which women span the boundary between family responsibilities and the wider world. However, it challenges accepted views that women care for children because their options are limited by expectations within society and the family that allow no other course of action. The research finds that many women actually welcome divided responsibilities and that for some, bounded contact with the outside world equates with choice.

This book exclusively studies women and the all-female nature of the research cohort, the educational, and the occupational contexts, embeds gender so deeply in the subtext that it is rendered almost invisible. Yet its effect on the women's lives is profound, as it underpins their desire to belong within the family, the community and wider society and mediates their freedom to choose. Gender is threaded through the data in a number of ways, in recounted actions, in spoken comments, in the constructs of caring and connectedness and the debates about emancipation and exploitation. It is also present in the overarching theoretical frameworks that we will use to make sense of the women's narratives, both established conceptualisations like the capability approach, and the newly developed theory of integrated lives.

Towards the end of this chapter the structure of the book is set out more fully, but a brief overview may be helpful here. *Women Studying Childcare* considers the historical context of education and childcare in England (in chapter 2) to set the scene, before moving on to explore the individual and collective accounts of women who use education to access work that fits the time and space, economic and social frameworks that shape their lives. It analyses their stories in a number of ways. It presents typologies that enable us to identify commonalities between individual life stories, furthering our knowledge of the childcare workforce (chapter 3), and offers theoretical perspectives that make sense of the students' choices and aspirations (chapter 4). It closely examines their actual narratives to identify their experiences prior to (chapter 5) and during (chapter 6) the study period. It then reports on the consequences of studying (chapter 7), before discussing the implications these hold for the students themselves and for wider society (chapter 8). Whenever possible the book uses the women's words directly, as this makes the biographies and anecdotes come alive, maintaining the polyvocal nature of this collective account even whilst I, the researcher and narrator, draw out the commonalities and differences hidden within the student narratives and consider their significance in policy terms.

From both a childcare and an adult education perspective, this is a story of stability and continuity, of gradual transition and orchestrated change; giving credence to Margaret Hodge's vision, as Minister for Education, of a 'silent revolution' in childcare at the start of the new millennium (Hodge, 2000). Many earlier studies of women's education aligned it with life change but this account of childcare workers tells a very different story. Developing a *theory of integrated lives* (see chapter 4), it reveals the care the women take to mesh together the different aspects of their lives and captures a general satisfaction with the pace of everyday life, which challenges the modernist notion that change equates with progress. Time to 'be' and to 'do' is important and the process of 'becoming' requires consideration and careful action, not least because many of the women are mothers and caring for their own children lies at the heart of their decision-making.

The women are choosing lives that minimise the conflict between their family, their workplace and their educational experiences and this is empowering for them, imbuing their stories with a liveliness and an overarching sense of achievement that contradicts oppressive accounts of childcare work. Without doubt working with young children in contemporary Britain is emotionally demanding and often it is lowly paid, but this need not mean that it is of a low standard or that it is carried out by people unable to find alternative employment. The mature women in this study come from a wide range of social and economic backgrounds and hold a broad range of qualifications. In addition to those with few or lower-level certification, many hold A-levels and university degrees. There are considerable variations in the time students stay in the profession and the levels of seniority they reach in childcare or related occupations, and this diversity is captured in a set of *occupational* and a set of *attitudinal typologies* (see chapter 3). These typologies contribute to an overall analysis that reveals there is no simple or predictable linear relationship between attainment and prior qualification or background. A significant number of additional characteristics (clearly laid out as capability indicators in chapter 4) play a part in determining outcomes for individuals including health and personal motivation but also opportunity – a factor that governments can directly address.

Women Studying Childcare discusses interview material offered by 33 students drawn flexibly but systematically from nine groups who, starting in 1997, enrolled in successive years. The overall cohort, which included a tenth group of completing students, numbered 170, of whom 150 students returned background questionnaires, enabling further verification of the interview data. All 150 students enrolled on a four-term Childcare Diploma in an English Further Education (FE) college over a ten-year period that roughly aligns with Tony Blair's New Labour government with its 'education, education, education' agenda and promise of a new 'learning age' (DfEE, 1998b). Thus, the study captures student reaction and opinion during a period of unprecedented educational change.

The interviews were carried out during 2006 and 2007. Students were asked to think back to their time on the Diploma and discuss their expectations, the practices encountered within education and the consequences they attributed to their period of study. They were also asked to talk in general terms about the purposes of education and their own experiences throughout the life-course. By leaving the selection of fine content to the students themselves, I was able to focus the research onto the aspects that were important to them, before lightly steering the interviews in directions of interest to me.

The students had all completed the *same* level 3 Diploma course in the *same* college taught by the *same* tutor, myself. This pre-existing relationship made it possible to carry out in-depth interviews in a single meeting, as I already knew each student quite well. It also enabled a thorough contextualisation of the research findings and a clear focus on the students themselves, as variations in the setting, the curriculum and teaching style were minimal over the ten-year period. I knew that I needed to avoid dominating the interviews but felt reassured that this was possible after reading Jennifer Nias's study *Primary Teachers Talking*. This dates from 1989 but is still relevant. In particular, I was influenced by her account of the research process in Walford's *Doing Educational Research*, where she claims: 'It did not take me long to realise that there was a mismatch between what they wanted to tell me and what I thought I wanted to know' (1991:148). Nias's account showed that talking to former students in a different context had the potential to reveal insights beyond those formed in the classroom and gave me the confidence to discard my interview questions and just let the students talk freely.

Through our shared experience as tutor and student we were able to develop a 'recall' method of interviewing whereby the students talked about their lives and educational experiences and I, as co-converser, questioned things that seemed contrived. I quickly learned to challenge hesitations, query contradictions and seek clarification of any uncertainties, developing the free-association interviewing techniques (cc) increasingly common in biographical studies and clearly outlined in Wendy Hollway and Tony Jefferson's book *Doing Qualitative Research Differently* (2000). The students and I were using our common memories to recall the past more accurately and to deepen our mutual understanding and this was immensely satisfying. Sometimes, however, when I read the interview transcripts later, it seemed as if I was making intuitive leaps in understanding. Keen to evidence my interpretation rather than leave it subjective I revisited the transcripts and found I could use the coding techniques that underpin conversation analysis (cc) to demonstrate how meaning is sometimes deduced from patterns within speech rather than from direct statements. As Paul Ten Have explains (1999), conversation analysis identifies the structures in speech by setting it out as a series of 'turns' and captures the nuances of language by marking pauses, stresses and changes of tone, pitch or volume. The codes look complicated on paper but are easily assimilated. Many readers will have used similar coding techniques when recording body language or turn taking during child observation.

Readers with an interest in research validity should note that I analysed the questionnaire material, collected from the entire cohort of 150, to establish the typicality of the in-depth accounts and to add corroborative explanatory material. Simple statistical comparisons demonstrated that the interview sample was indeed representative of the overall cohort. In both, approximately half of the students worked in the voluntary sector, around 6 to 7 per cent in the private sector and 15 per cent in the state sector, more commonly in primary than nursery classes. Slightly more than 10 per cent worked in other, related, fields and a small number no longer worked in childcare at the time of interview. Similarly, both groups were equally divided into managers and assistant staff. In terms of family structure, the majority of students were married (80%) and more than 70 per cent were currently living with young children. Also, most worked part-time for a salary not much higher than the national minimum wage.

A comparison with *Labour Force Survey* data for 2001-05 (Simon *et al*, 2007) demonstrates that, if the under-25 category is excluded from that survey, the students in this book share many of the national characteristics of the child-care workforce in England; particularly in being 'overwhelmingly female and white', although this study does include a small number of mainland European and Asian participants. Within a qualitative study further comparison is speculative, but the statistical parallels suggest that the interview data bears a degree of national typicality so readers of this account can be confident that other students will hold similar views. This claim is important, as some of the classic studies of childcare trainees do not fully consider mature student cohorts. The studies are still, quite rightly, highly regarded but have led to generalised views of childcare training and work that are selective, generating stereotypes of carers that need to be challenged.

The training of mature childcare staff has its own distinctive pattern. The stories I am about to tell stand apart from earlier works on further education and from studies of women in higher education where students often seek a life-change. This book is not about the 'largely unqualified army' of childcare and education workers described by Hevey and Curtis (1996:212) but about those women who, for whatever reason, chose to attain a level three supervisory qualification. Neither is this a study of young women training to work in 'care', as described by Beverley Skeggs in her sociological study *Formations of Class and Gender*, a 1997 updating of research carried out in the early 1980s. The majority of Skeggs' students were enrolled full-time in vocational training, studying social care rather than childcare, so without the educational elements important to a childcare syllabus. They were almost exclusively working class and seeking 'respectability': not characteristics that apply to the mature students. Nor does the study evoke Helen Colley's work on childcare students. These too were younger, full-time trainees being schooled by trainers who themselves had been habituated into promoting appropriate values. I recognise the behaviours that Colley describes: the process whereby tutors 'immersed in the vocational culture themselves' seek to enculture new trainees (Colley *et al*, 2003:490). I have worked with many colleagues who fit the stereotype but also with others who do not.

The historical traditions of childcare training are discussed further in chapter 2 but here I must stress that many of the trainers of mature women enter the profession after earlier careers, and have a broad range of higher level qualifications and experiences. The pattern of career change described within this study anticipates the *Early Years Professional Status* (EYPS) (cc) initiative of the new millennium more closely than it echoes the stereotype described by Colley. Perhaps I can make this clearer by briefly describing my credentials, as my own career path is one of conversion. I am a geography graduate who carried out archival research in Mexico before settling to a career in publishing, achieving managing editor status before choosing to work freelance. Like many of the students whom I have trained, I became interested in early years education when my children were small, volunteering in a local pre-school before deciding to qualify. Over a period of more than twenty years I undertook a series of paid and voluntary roles, working in settings and in advisory capacities and acquiring relevant qualifications, teaching in community, further and then higher education. Childcare – or, less succinctly, early years education – was very much a second career focus, supported by my prior experiences and qualifications. I consider myself 'educated' and 'educator', committed to meeting students' needs and listening to their opinions, rather than to inculcating a narrow vision of childcare work.

I was, and am, genuinely interested in the students' lives, fascinated by the stories they tell and the patterns within those narratives. I also find the research process enthralling, rejoicing in the opportunity to let the students speak for themselves; and it is this open-minded approach that led me to some original conclusions. Rejecting set interview schedules and computerised analysis as too mechanical, I settled instead for flexibility – engaging in interactive conversation, typing the transcripts in their entirety to ensure a complete analysis, and immersing myself in the material until patterns and connections began to appear.

I soon began to notice distinctive types of behaviour. Some students repeated similar actions throughout their life-course. Focusing closely on these actions, I identified similar if less-marked patterns in the behaviour of other students, eventually leading to the typologies described in chapter 3. Groups of students displayed distinctive patterns of activity suggesting the attitudinal typologies of accepter, agoniser, accumulater and asserter. Students also displayed differing levels of commitment to childcare work and these I could make sense of through the occupational typologies of sampler, stager, settler, switcher and step-upper. These categories, and the iterative processes of defining and refining them, gave me a sense of some control of the data and some confidence that the research might increase our knowledge of motivation within the childcare workforce.

A retrospective discussion like this disguises the struggle the researcher has with raw data. The process of sense-making is neither easy nor linear but this only increases the pleasure in those eureka moments when meanings become clear. I spent a great deal of time trying to separate the students' educational material from other aspects of their narratives before eventually realising it was impossible. The research data was telling me something entirely different and when I started to listen closely I made a theoretical breakthrough. Education was important to the students; it underpinned their stories about their own childhoods and their children, their parents and parental expectations, their experiences before, around and after the Diploma and their plans for the future. Yet education was not a distinct strand in their lives but a facilitative – occasionally negative – element, closely meshed with their discourses on family and work. It shaped their choices and empowered their actions. Understanding this led me to the theorisation described in chapter 4. The *triple triangle that maintains integrated lives* defines the connections the students forge between their familial, educational and vocational activities and the embedded reciprocal relationships between education, family and work. This triangle supports a level of stability in their lives that explains the students' satisfaction, despite economic and time constraints, and reveals the importance of detailed qualitative research that examines the minutiae of life.

A holistic analysis noted the student's focus on the present; plans for the future were discussed but with no immediacy. Students were generally content with life in the present and it was this focus on current *being* and *doing* that caused me to recognise the relevance of the *capability approach* (CA) to my own research. This is a conceptualisation occasionally used in education, in particular by Michael Watts, Melanie Walker and Elaine Unterhalter, whose key works are listed in the references. The capability approach (cc) (described in detail in chapter 4) is a theoretical framework devised over several decades by Nobel prize-winning economist Amartya Sen (see Sen, 1999 for an overview).

Sen is concerned with the quality of life, hence the focus on the present rather than exclusively on long-term goals. His work offers insights into choice and inequality with regard to public policy. Sen believes that policy-makers too often offer a single 'preferable' outcome rather than a range of options that might allow people to make personalised choices geared to their own needs. Sen recognises that choice is neither random (where anything is possible) nor rational (with a single, predictable, optimum preference), but bounded. Each individual has a *capability set* (cc), a number of possible options, some of which they could choose to implement.

Chapter 4 shows that the triple triangle can be construed as a typical capability set for mature women training in childcare since it represents the structural framework within which the students can make co-realisable choices. This connection makes the theorisation more powerful but also, reciprocally, enables the research data to be used to develop aspects of capability theory. Analysis reveals common factors that affect individual students' longer-term achievements and these are recast as capability indicators and linked together to form chains. Importantly, co-comparison of these capability chains highlights the need to listen to individual stories and draw out the common meanings, rather than to isolate different qualities like class or qualification and make assumptions from such characteristics. The stories told in this book clearly show that disposition and opportunity combine to facilitate a range of individual outcomes that could not be anticipated from background characteristics. Life is indeed more complex than some large-scale extrapolative studies suggest.

Chapters 5, 6 and 7 analyse the student interviews in detail, considering themes that are common across the narratives. They draw in turn on the student accounts of their educational expectations, the practices they encountered, and the consequences of studying, both anticipated and actual. The students describe their attitudes to education in their own words, demonstrating both similarities of expression and belief and also distinctive variations. They reveal how the boundaries between education, work and family are blurred, with education often occupying the spaces remaining after other commitments have been met, making it both a marginalised and a luxury activity. Chapter 8 considers the students' needs and strengths in a broader context, examining in particular their contribution to the local communities in which they live and less directly, to society in general. In policy terms, it draws attention to the dangers inherent in exponential change that narrowly pursues focused objectives in the name of progress. Whereas grass-roots movements develop ecologically, top down initiatives risk cutting across existing structures that work for the good of society.

The discussion above offers a flavour of the emergent methodology used in the initial study, one in which understanding surfaced slowly during the research processes. My original doctoral thesis started with a detailed examination of the data and slowly built up to a theoretical overview, but here the theoretical positions are explored first and this chapter discusses the focus and audience and summarises the overall content. Chapter 2 considers the historical, social and political context, stressing the contemporary pattern of change. Chapter 3 describes the two typologies: occupational and attitudinal. Chapter 4 presents the triple triangle maintaining integrated lives, exploring a range of supportive theory and the connections with the capability approach. Chapter 5 considers students' prior experiences and their expectations on enrolling on the Diploma, chapter 6 their discussion of educational practices, and chapter 7 the consequences of studying from both close and wider perspectives. Chapter 8 summarises the main arguments and teases out the implications for childcare and broader society, drawing attention to women's needs and their strengths.

The book concludes with a *concept catalogue*, a specialised glossary that defines and offers further sources for the many ideas derived from sociology, psychology and economics; concepts that often appear in educational books without adequate explanation.

2

Putting policy in perspective

Women Studying Childcare straddles the boundaries of adult, vocational and women's, education. In terms of content, the childcare element connects to developments in compulsory education. Therefore, we need to look across the different sectors and briefly consider the historical and social contexts of education, its piecemeal development, its diversity of purpose and its dominant discourses. We examine how the story of integrated lives emerges from a long historical tradition of women taking responsibility for children, whether this is chosen or enforced and whether training in childcare is emancipatory or exploitative in practice. Finally we look at the current political context, identifying a stream of policy initiatives that demonstrate the exponential nature of the recent changes in early years education in England, anticipating the women's concerns, voiced later in the book.

Whether we focus on compulsory, adult or nursery-level provision, we can trace similarities. In all these fields, the picture is of fragmented development, social inequality, and limited public funding alongside private investment, philanthropic endeavour and voluntarism: a *laissez-faire* approach partly disguised in the early years sector by the recent grouping together of private, voluntary and independent settings, as a single PVI sector. Successive British governments have failed to take full responsibility for the educational system in terms of either funding or practices and new initiatives have tended to add to rather than replace existing provision.

We saw this in 1870 when Forster's Education Act made elementary education compulsory and state provision was added piecemeal to an existing array of church, charity and 'dame' schools and home-based tutoring systems. We saw it again in 1965 when comprehensive schooling was introduced, without legislation, to challenge existing patterns of grammar school provision. It is evident in the early years sector, where the vision of a national network of children's centres has seen the renaming and partial redevelopment of many existing nurseries and pre-schools alongside the expansion of private day nurseries. Ironically, it is this partial reconstruction of existing provision, often disparaged as 'patchy', that preserves a continuing element of choice but disguises the reality that for many, choice is dictated by circumstances. Accessibility, costs and attitudes can seriously reduce options.

The merits of a single integrated educational system are frequently debated but rarely upheld in practice. We continue to separate out higher, further and skills education even though, with different labels, the tripartite division (cc) into liberal, vocational and radical purposes has been traced back to ancient Greece, to Plato's division of society into rulers, auxiliaries and other workers (Lea *et al*, 2003). Thus, we perpetuate the division of society along class lines and constrain educational practices by narrowly defining goals. This separation of liberal, vocational and radical values creates instability, as policy can be manipulated to serve these different ends and to value one over another. In times of financial downturn, vocational and skills-based learning are favoured and financed, but this practice actually perpetuates existing divisions within society as those who can afford a liberal education can still pursue it whilst the least well-off are channelled into a vocational route.

At present, education both nationally and globally, has an instrumental orientation as governments strive to improve economic prosperity by raising qualification levels within the workforce. The swing towards vocational education in Britain is traceable to James Callaghan's *Great Debate* speech of 1976. In favouring the less qualified in society, this move appears to serve a social justice agenda but in maintaining the division of educational purpose within society it actually perpetuates social division, and this is cause for concern. In *The Spirit Level* (2009) Richard Wilkinson and Kate Pickett provide thirty years of statistical evidence to demonstrate that unequal societies disadvantage everyone who lives in them.

Thus, in the maintenance of separate liberal, vocational and radical strands, education remains a force for social control. Frank Furedi believes that control is embedded in other ways too. In *The Therapy Culture* (cc) he argues that the current focus on emotional intelligence 'extends the business of government from the public to the private and more disturbingly to the internal life of the individual' (2004:198). He expresses concern that the 'institutionalisation of the therapeutic ethos' serves to enforce compliance and conformity and dependence on the state for help and support, so decreasing people's sense of agency, and argues against teachers crossing the boundary between education and 'instructing pupils how to feel' (*ibid*:197).

Kathryn Ecclestone and Dennis Hayes apply Furedi's ideas across the educational spectrum, in their book, *The Dangerous Rise of Therapeutic Education* (2009). They argue that the focus on personal skills and emotions is undermining the knowledge purposes of education, creating a dependent and dependable workforce in support of national economic goals. This argument may have relevance in the compulsory sector but seems contrived within early years, where the care element is fundamental and where encouraging verbal and social skills has primary significance. The therapeutic culture is also refuted within adult education. Veronica McGivney (2005) argues that humanist traditions have long prevailed in this sector and tutors customarily support the individual's personal goals alongside his or her academic learning.

Adult educators are accustomed to creating safe environments, or 'protected enclaves' for their students but are increasingly feeling the strain of keeping the audit trail at bay as pressures to demonstrate efficiency and efficacy increase. Sociologist Pamela Broadfoot (1999) likens such managerialist (cc) interventions to a Foucauldian form of panoptic surveillance (cc) where protective self-monitoring ensures total monitoring. Broadfoot claims that both staff and students are managed through a series of micro-penalties aimed at maintaining compliance. For students, this is a system of grading and reports; for staff, paper trails and feedback responses that 'measure' whether they are carrying out their duties properly. Students and staff are thus set up to manage each other, for the staff grade the students and the students feed back their satisfaction whereas managers simply monitor the results. Thus, education again becomes a form of social control.

Within women's education, issues of social control are evident but contestable. The literature offers no clear answer to the question of whether caring for children is emancipative or oppressive. It can be claimed (after David, 1980) that in earlier times women were educated to civilise sons and husbands, so mothers were part of the control system. At the same time, however, there is a case that the ideology of family maintains women's subordinate position (Barrett and McIntosh, 1982; cited by Smart, 2007). Here too is a system of reciprocal surveillance. Plus there is an element of class control. Skeggs (1997) draws parallels between the training of working-class girls for the caring professions and earlier patterns of indoctrination of domestic servants. In both practices, middle-class women taught and insisted on 'appropriate' standards of behaviour from working-class girls, stabilising society along class lines. These consequences of education are all oppressive. Furthermore, some feminists consider training women to work in childcare to be exploitative as it facilitates a move from an *unpaid* to an *underpaid* occupation (Clarke, 2002). Certainly, when we examine the student accounts we need to bear in mind Skeggs' claim (1997) that caring for others requires an abnegation of self and also the widespread view, building on Diane Reay's (2000) identification of emotional capital (cc), that the skills that are central to caring are not adequately recompensed. The contemporary discussion of professionalism in early years education emphasises the need to take its female qualities into account. Jayne Osgood (2006b:194), for example, requires us to seek a 'viable alternative construction of professionalism, which encapsulates and maintains an ethics of care and, at the same time, is infused with pride, confidence and self-belief'.

It is plausible, nevertheless, that the longer historical perspective supports the emancipative over the exploitative view. Educating women for domesticity or to bring up children was initially progressive. As historian Margaret Bryant (1985) explains, it offered women an education when previously they had none. Similarly the role of governess allowed single women to support themselves financially. Ruth Watts (2000:41) claims that for middle-class women 'not rich enough to be unemployed', teaching was the only respectable option.

In offering teacher training, Froebel's kindergartens were seen to be 'enlarging the scope of women's fundamental rights and professional opportunities' (Brosterman 1997:93); a point affirmed by Kevin Brehony (2000:183) who tells us that 'at least one of its participants regarded it as part of the women's movement ... because it supported and enabled middle-class women to gain employment'. Brehony draws connections between the kindergarten movement and the Socialist settlements set up to encourage educated individuals to live among the poor to exchange cultural expectations. Citing Martha Vicinus, he claims that those in women's settlements 'were determined to turn philanthropy into a paid profession' (*ibid*:189) suggesting, by association, that childcare work may well have been emancipatory for women as well as children. He reminds us that 'the Froebel movement was composed overwhelmingly of women' and this in itself suggests a degree of agency (*ibid*:183).

Vicinus herself (1985:218) describes the McMillan sisters, founders of the open-air schools, as 'deeply influenced by the newer ideologies of Socialism' but also the Christian vision of a better future for all. The Montessori system also created a demand for 'properly trained personnel' (Cunningham, 2000) and, like the Steiner nursery movement, organised its own courses for teachers. More recently, ventures like the Pre-school Learning Alliance (set up as the Pre-school Playgroups Association in 1961) and the High-Scope Foundation also offered specialised training in childcare.

Significantly, the Pre-school Learning Alliance was an organisation set up by mothers that trained parents to work with children. This marks a move towards training and employing women who have children, as well as those who are childless, enabling the mothers of small children to enter part-time work. Therefore, when we view the recurring pattern of women working in part-time childcare establishments as a marginal pursuit we should remember that this may represent a step towards, rather than away from, independence. Historically the consequences of women's education, like many real world outcomes, contained contradictory positive and negative elements.

Entering the debate at this level, however, obscures the more basic assumptions underpinning a gendered society (cc, gender). To many feminists, women's relegation to the domestic, private sphere (cc) is a violation of their human rights. Even to the less ardent, it is clear that society is unequally divided on gendered lines. A Marxist sociological view aligns the division of labour within the family with the development of capitalism in post-industrial Britain. To simplify the argument (described by, among others, Mechthild Hart, 1992): in urbanised industrial society, male labour moved out of the home and into factories and mills in exchange for a regular wage. Housework and childcare remained within the family dwelling and, having no monetary value, acquired a supportive rather than a true economic status. This led to more general inequalities as salaried men, working specified hours and freed of caring responsibilities, were able to engage in political and social activity in the wider community, the public sphere (cc), whereas women bore all the domestic responsibilities.

In his discussions of the capability approach (cc), Amartya Sen, and his sometimes co-writer, Martha Nussbaum, recognise the inequality inherent in policy that treats the household as the basic unit of measurement and distribution. Family and societal groupings often disguise the disadvantage of some constituent members, particularly women and children, whose poorer treatment in impoverished families may disappear from sight in statistics that focus on heads of households or family units. The capability approach is predominately concerned with the lesser-developed world but Sen (1999:89) questions the 'presumption – often implicitly made' that gender inequality does not apply to Western countries. Nussbaum, a feminist philosopher, describes the problem graphically:

> The damage women suffer in the family takes a particular form: the woman is treated not as an end in herself, but as an adjunct or instrument of the needs of others, as a mere reproducer, cook, cleaner, sexual outlet, caretaker, rather than as a source of agency and worth in her own right. (Nussbaum, 2000:243)

These arguments build up a view of women and their education as peripheral to mainstream society. Much adult educational provision shares this characteristic. In many instances it remains localised and marginalised in terms of the hours (often evening classes), locations (in community rooms and educational establishments when the core students are off site) and, more importantly, political power. Although the pattern of marginal location was not true for the level 3 Diploma course on which this study focuses, it was typical for pre-qualificatory childcare courses. However, we should see this as both strength and weakness as evening classes in nearby community rooms often suit the parents of young children, who rely on friends or partners for baby-sitting and are unable or unwilling to travel far from home.

The predominance of women in adult education both creates and promotes marginality. Childcare work, and training too, is mostly female. In 1997 when the first study cohort enrolled, male students accounted for only 1 per cent of those in training (Penn and McQuail, 1997) and in 2001 Cameron, Owen and Moss maintained that there had been 'no change in the gender balance employed in nurseries in over ten years' (p72): it is still 99 per cent female overall. Despite national efforts to improve this statistic only 'around' 2 per cent of the workforce were male by the end of 2008 according to the *Times Educational Supplement* (Ward, 2009). This segregation facilitates the continuance of feminine practices within the profession. Cameron, Moss and Owen's (1999) study *Men in the Nursery* found evidence that feminised traditions, based on a 'motherhood model' of care that women took for granted, often excluded men even while they were overtly welcomed, and that gender issues were rarely discussed and customarily hidden within a discourse of individuality. On a positive note, however, parents were found to be open-minded about the gender identity of staff members and this could operate as a driver for change.

The governments of both main political parties have demonstrated a commitment to creating change in the early years sector, with a scope that is much broader than issues of gender equality. This interest in the early years is relatively recent, perhaps long overdue but certainly exponential in its rate of impact. We have seen that the sector was slow to develop. Apart from isolated initiatives – Robert Owen's experimental nursery school at the New Lanark Mills in 1816 is a well-documented example – formal education for young children was practically non-existent. Even in the late 19th and early 20th centuries, nursery provision was limited. Quasi-private, semi-philanthropical initiatives of church and charitable institutions played a pioneering role, as did individual Socialists like the McMillan sisters. The Froebel, Montessori and, on a smaller scale, the Steiner-Waldorf foundations developed both child-centred educational theories and institutions in which to apply their beliefs, training specialist staff to educate the young. But the impact of these pioneers in Britain was limited, as their efforts received little official support. Tricia David (1990:19) claims that by 1900, some 43 per cent of 3- to 5-year-olds attended private kindergartens, nurseries or board schools but children were often in classes with one teacher for 60 children, necessitating formal approaches. Provision targeted those perceived to need it. In 1938, the UK boasted 118 nursery schools, mainly catering for working-class children, and 104 day nurseries, *caring* for children from problem families and for those whose parents worked full-time (*ibid*:20,10).

Nursery provision rose and fell during the war years as the state called upon the 'reserve army' of female labour. The intention of the 1944 Education Act that all local authorities should establish nursery schools was never enforced, nor funded. From 1961, with the foundation of the pre-school movement, voluntary groups began to fill the gap, beginning with play and gradually introducing learning through play. Formal changes were few, even though the Plowden Report (CACE, 1967), supported the notion of universal nursery education, and the White Paper *Education: a framework for expansion* (DES, 1972) recommended the expansion of nursery provision within schools.

Where local authorities did act, the tendency was to place 4-year-old children in reception classes with older children rather than create special provision. This practice was noted in the White Paper *Better Schools* (DES, 1985) but described as a 'relatively new phenomenon' by the British Association for Early Childhood Education (BAECE) in the mid-80s (McCail, c1986). Concerns for 4-year-olds in school were widely voiced in this period. The Royal Commission on *Achievement in Primary Schools* (HMSO, 1986) acknowledged the problem but, recognising economic constraints, sought to improve conditions in infant classes rather than endorse nursery expansion. The Royal Commission requested and triggered further research into appropriate provision: by BAECE (McCail, c1986) and the National Foundation for Education Research (NFER, 1987; Cleave and Brown, c1989; Brown and Cleave, 1994). The debate became entangled with that of school start dates and the relative importance of care and education for young children. It was only in the late 1980s and 1990s with the advent of educare (cc) that the UK made real attempts to overcome a pattern that was 'more clearly divided yet more complex than that in other European countries' (David, 1990:17) and merge the caring and educational traditions within childcare.

It is likely that both external and internal pressures directed attention to the education of the young. Internally, the Education Reform Act of 1988, in re-modelling the primary and secondary curricula, afforded business interests the capacity to exert influence beyond the compulsory sector. Externally, the 1989 United Nations Convention on the Rights of the Child, implemented in the UK through the Children Act 1989, challenged the dependent status of children and privileged their needs over those of the family, reinforcing the care element.

In the early 1990s, four reports on early years provision were published in rapid succession. Privately commissioned reports, *Start Right: the importance of early learning* (Ball, 1994) and *Learning to Succeed* (National Commission on Education, 1993 and the Paul Hamlyn Foundation) were neatly sandwiched by the official Rumbold Report, *Starting with Quality* (DES, 1990) and *Counting to Five: education of children under five* (Audit Commission for England and Wales, 1996). Together, these prompted the Conservative government in 1996 to introduce an element of state funding, through a nursery voucher scheme, and an early years curriculum based on 'desirable learning outcomes' (SCAA, 1996) to ensure appropriate standards of provision.

On election in 1997 the Labour government made only minor changes to Conservative policies, introducing capitation and establishing the 'early learning goals' that were later codified as a *Curriculum Guidance* framework for England (QCA, 2000); voluntary in 2000, statutory in 2002. However, in enacting devolution (1998) the government supported differential imple-mentation of national strategies so in this book, policy is described from a predominantly English perspective. The *National Childcare Strategy* of May 1998, introduced through the Green Paper *Meeting the Childcare Challenge* (DfEE, 1998a), set (unrealised) goals for staff training and the *National Quali-fication Framework* of 1999 led to some degree of standardisation of content and assessment (through performance criteria) in many childcare courses. The *National Standards for Childcare* (DfEE, 2001) established that 50 per cent of staff must be qualified and incorporated the legal requirements for settings into a single document, with government funding consequent upon satisfactory inspection by the Ofsted Early Years Directorate. The publication of *Birth to Three Matters* (Sure Start Unit, 2002) endorsed the need to plan learning activities for younger children, but not in a way that encouraged curriculum coherence across sectors.

The Children Act 2004 (cc) heralded more significant and co-ordinated changes: the revolution was no longer 'silent'. This Act implemented the *Every Child Matters* (DfES, 2003, cc) outcomes for children under 5. More controversially, it established the national children's database (switched off in August 2010), and allowed the extension of parenting orders to enforce attendance at parenting classes, demonstrating significant intervention in areas previously considered private. Major restructuring led to the integration of education and social care services and the establishment of Children's Trusts with a Director of Children's Services in each local authority and a national Children's Director. The 2006 Childcare Act provided the legislative basis for Sure Start children's centres in each local authority and the implementation in September 2008 of the new Early Years Foundation Stage (DfES, 2007, cc). This co-ordinated provision for children from 0 to 5, codifying the curriculum and care standards. The *Children's Plan* (DCSF, 2007:2) identified progress over the previous ten years and set out an agenda for continuing improvement 'to make England the best place in the world for children and young people'.

The reform agenda supported the cause of working families through the *Ten Year Strategy for Parents* (HM Treasury, 2004) and the 2006 Childcare Act (cc) that formalised the parental right to high quality services led by qualified staff. The *Children's Workforce Strategy* of 2005 established plans to improve and administer flexible training options, a responsibility passed to the Children's Workforce Development Council (CWDC) from 2006. The *Early Years Professional Status* (EYPS, cc) initiative of June 2006, was a key new development intended to encourage both the training and importation of graduates and break the pattern of in-house training that led to a continual recycling of poor or moderate practice. It also began to address the issue of appropriate remuneration for higher qualified staff. However, there is some concern that policy initiatives risk-recreating a two-tier workforce: those who care and those who educate. The introduction of a single *Diploma for Children and Young People* in 2010 limits choice and may, like earlier National Vocational Qualifications (NVQs), 'keep workers in the estate to which their employers have called them' (Wolf, 2009). The course uses task-based assessment that offers no means of demonstrating higher levels of understanding so cannot support graduate entry. Nor is it likely to equip students with the skills they need for further study. As I write, these issues are leading to a reconsideration of the award and possibly the addition of extension units.

These significant policy initiatives were accompanied by many changes to the names of structures and personnel, mirrored at national levels in the repeated renaming and regrouping of government departments, partly a facet of multi-agency working. Uncertainty stemming from this shifting policy background was further exacerbated by the change of government in May 2010 and also its coalition status. It is scarcely surprising that practitioners, trainers, and parents alike struggle to keep up with new initiatives and to develop a body of tacit knowledge to inform their decisions. We see that students often find it frustrating that their learning becomes dated almost as soon as they qualify, and that some early years groups rely on enrolling successive students on courses just to have someone who is currently up-to-date.

Overall, the new policy initiatives induced stress and uncertainty when they were imposed, from above, on a sector developing from a series of grass-roots movements with a long tradition of voluntarism. The pre-school sector in this study is largely run by mothers who are willing to train to care for other people's children alongside their own, rather than detached professionals fully accustomed to the public sphere and less personal forms of interaction. The later chapters show that it is often the conflict between what should happen and what does happen that creates the tensions and stresses that the women mention. First though, chapters 3 and 4 show how the women's ways of working create frameworks that enable them to withstand such stresses, and how these explain the overall levels of satisfaction that emanate from their accounts of their lives.

3
Committing to a career
in childcare

In this chapter we see how the historical trend of mature women training to work with children continues but is subtly changed when provision is community-based, so enabling local involvement. For many, particularly women who have children, childcare is not necessarily a permanent career nor is it the only choice available to them. Rather, it is an occupation that suits their immediate needs and desires, allowing for the role of motherhood but opening up further opportunities for those who are motivated to seek them out. As this chapter shows, for many women their immediate future depends on their sense of agency and the extent to which they embrace the opportunities offered within the childcare profession.

The research interviews revealed that the women's decisions to work and train in childcare were often reactive rather than proactive and grew out of their experience of mothering. Only three students (Greta, Hansa and Imogen) were childless. The majority were parents who had volunteered in their children's pre-schools as committee members or as casual workers. Almost two thirds had been parent helpers before being encouraged by their pre-school experience to undertake training. Sometimes they enrolled after a part-time job was offered (26 were employed before commencing the Diploma course), sometimes in anticipation that a job might arise. Sometimes they talked to other parents who had enjoyed a childcare course, and registered because it sounded interesting. Irma enrolled simply because her friend was doing it: 'Can't see why not. It's not full time. I've only got to work two mornings at pre-school and go back to college'.

This pattern places family as the starting point for a childcare career for mature students, paid or voluntary work as the common second element, and education as the means of facilitating this progression. It demonstrates that the students were seeking education not primarily for instrumental gain but to protect and develop what they already had, showing how family and community ties clearly influenced their decisions.

I noted, too, that there were patterns in the ways individual students engaged with childcare work. Some drifted along, some planned ahead, some actively shaped the environment to suit their own needs, some stayed a short while and others developed permanent careers. Seeking to make sense of these tendencies I eventually realised that I was looking at two different types of engagement. One related only to childcare and typified student's commitment to the profession. These could be codified as a set of occupational typologies. The other related more broadly to the students' dispositions, describing patterns of behaviour that became visible in the more biographical sections of the interviews as they reoccurred in different contexts. These could be codified as a set of attitudinal typologies.

The typologies (see table 1) permit meaningful grouping, enabling some detailed insights into everyday life; perhaps even a degree of generalisability from a mass of real world data that is highly individualised. They were compiled from a combination of direct and indirect evidence. With the occupational typology, sometimes a student clearly stated an intention or affiliation, eg 'I just fell into childcare' or 'I worked as a hairdresser for ten years'. Other situations required a broader analysis to determine significance. For example, when a student had five unrelated casual jobs over six years, I took this to indicate a lack of identifiable career structure prior to entering childcare. With the attitudinal typology it was necessary to seek out a range of supporting evidence, as claims for particular dispositional characteristics could only be deemed valid if consistently present in a narrative.

It was possible to allocate all 33 interviewees to a category in each set of typologies (see appendix). Only in a few (identified) cases was it difficult to make definitive attributions and for these students alternative categories are also included to demonstrate plurality. The classifications are based upon summative decisions made in a single moment, and students may over time move from one category to another. Also, despite the exclusivity of the categories, some students change category if they alter their beliefs, behaviour or work-practices; others straddle the boundaries. When analysing the entire interview sample, there were people who were currently resting between

Table 1: Taxonomy of typologies

Occupational typologies (Outcome-related categories)	
Sampler	One who drifted into childcare, found it lacking and quickly moved on
Stager	One who found childcare work convenient when the children were small
Settler	One who chose childcare as a career after experiencing a range of alternatives
Switcher	One who chose childcare as an alternative career to a previous one
Step-upper	One using childcare work to access an associated, better paid position/career
Attitudinal typologies (Process-related categories)	
Accepter	One with a relaxed, opportunistic approach; a reactive decision-maker
Agoniser	One who reflects intensely before making decisions; may analyse guilt
Accumulater	One who steadily acquires qualifications and experiences; maybe with a focus
Asserter	One with goal-oriented behaviour; a striver to 'get on'

jobs; those caught at a time of flux when it was impossible to guess where and if they would move on; and some individuals, like Irma, who demonstrated a mix of characteristics. In relation to childcare she displays characteristics of a *stager*, doing the course 'while I'm at home trying to have another baby, sort of thing'. However, her entire employment career renders her also a *sampler*. Despite a more sustained period running a garage franchise, she had tried – and walked away from – eight other casual jobs before she tried childcare.

The typologies are now discussed and related to an individual student narrative.

Occupational typologies

The outcome categories were determined from students' employment history pre- and post-Diploma. The significant characteristics are consistency, commitment and achievement.

Samplers

Samplers are people who experienced working in childcare, found that it did not suit them, and swiftly moved on to something else. Often, but not always, students drifted into the work because it was available, frequently because friends were already so employed. Reasons for not settling ranged from the personal ('I've got a very weak stomach') and concerns about the money ('I'm worth more than £6 an hour'), to feeling undervalued ('It would have been nice if they said Yes, you do work hard'), so mostly they were negatively associated with childcare. The core criterion for this category is that the students had never really developed a commitment to childcare, because negative opinions were occasionally expressed by students who nevertheless decided to remain in the field.

Greta is definitely a sampler of childcare work. It is an occupation that she tries, finds frustrating, and rejects. The sampling pattern is apparent in her earlier approaches to life, as she has drifted into one activity after another without making a long-term commitment. There is, however, a strong caring theme that underpins all her work. She constantly seeks a Utopian society where people matter more than budgets; possibly because of her own educational experiences in a 'dame' school (cc), and later in a rough secondary, where no one cared enough. Her story is a restless one, for she is a person who seeks more than life has given her. She is very reflective, demonstrating agoniser characteristics, but sufficiently self-aware to assert herself on occasion.

Disliking retail work, she remedied her earlier educational deficits and demonstrated a surprising survival instinct by forging her father's signature to procure a college place to study for O- and A-levels; an action more characteristic of an asserter. She then proceeded to a degree. All her decision-making processes reveal a trial-and-error structure. She tried three FE colleges before finding one that was right and enrolled on first one and then another degree course before graduating successfully, following advice to study history rather than her own inclination to study sociology.

Greta drifted into work in a job centre, having initially applied for work as a cleaner. Given responsibility for long-term unemployed, sex offenders, and ex-servicemen, she turned this into a caring role, holding jobs back for the needy and visiting them at home, unofficially, to inform them of new opportunities. When Restart interviews made this work less people-friendly she took a job in a centre for adults with learning difficulties, again becoming disillusioned when financial cuts and the 'push to get people more out into the community' altered the nature of the work. Family and relationship issues led to further moves, in both employment and geographical terms. She tried escort work, bussing children with special educational needs to school, and then began work in an after-school club. This was a reactive decision: she was 'really at a loss and a friend along the road said how they needed an extra person where she worked'.

Personal circumstances enforced a further geographical move and seeking work, she 'ended up doing the same job here'. The after-school club experience led to work in a pre-school and for a while she 'did the two jobs together', giving up the after-school club when she became unhappy with their working practices. However, she finds the paperwork 'really stressful' and no longer wants to work in the group as 'humanity gets lost' when the focus is on observing and documenting children rather than simply caring for them. She plans to move into gardening after her next house move, rather than childcare.

> I feel that I have come to a dead end now in the job at the playgroup because I just feel it is drudgery now.

Some of Greta's restlessness stems from the recent loss of both her parents. But she is someone who thinks deeply about issues and cares immensely for others. She admits 'it's horrible to think about your past' but her rationalisation of her life story shows that she has done this in detail and analytically. Perhaps because she cares so deeply, she finds it difficult to find a permanent niche in our far-from-perfect world.

Stagers

Stagers set out with the intention of finding, or recognised the convenience of, work that accommodated their own children's and families' needs in terms of hours and holidays. They made it clear that childcare work was a short-term option and that, once their children were older, they intended to find other means of earning their living. Sometimes they returned to earlier occupations, sometimes they sought new arenas. Working in childcare was thus defined as something to do while the children were little.

Typical is Diane, who says of pre-school work: 'I'd always given myself five years'. She has no doubt that her childcare work centred round her own children's needs:

> I gave up work so I could be at home to look after the children. That was more important than earning money.

Despite her intention, it is clear that Diane's actual decision to move on was triggered by her home *and* work situation. She explains that her husband's redundancy was making life 'tricky' and hints at problems in the workplace due to her preference for playing with the children rather than managing the setting. For her, early years work 'was becoming a little too regimented'. She was demonstrably disillusioned with childcare work. She recalls an embarrassing first interview with a potential employer, at which 'everything really came out about the way I was feeling'.

What is unusual about Diane, who professes to 'enjoy learning so much', is that she definitely sees education as set apart from real life. She claims that she 'entered life' when she graduated in geography. On seeking careers advice after pre-school work, she talks about it being 'fifteen years since the real world'. She tells of the adviser warning her she would have a 'real mountain to climb' to get back into work, strengthening the notion that she was changing career. She states that 'it hasn't been easy, making the change because it's, you know, it's almost taking one career and then stopping it and starting a new career'.

It is noteworthy that Diane treats her childcare work as a career because before she had children she had not used this term to describe the jobs she took wherever her husband worked. Perhaps this is because they were very varied in nature, demonstrating her accepter characteristics: management trainee in a retail organisation, working on an archaeological site, publishing for a learned society, and local authority work in the housing department and later in 'rented property in another county'.

Diane is able to use aspects of her childcare education in her new post: largely generic topics relating to community support, health and safety, diversity and equal opportunities. She is working for a quango where her geographical skills are also useful so it could be said that she has found a new career that draws on all her strengths. She has stepped up – but not within childcare.

Settlers
Most settlers had tried a range of different jobs before entering childcare but once they found work in the sector, they appeared to be ready to establish a childcare career. Settlers might move from one setting to another but they do so opportunistically rather than in pursuit of 'getting on', demonstrating an underlying permanence in their occupational choice. They are usually aware of, and to some degree accept, the career's limitations. Some decide to study further to broaden their possible childcare careers, and may even consider

progress into teaching or management at a later date (becoming step-uppers) but these changes are approached in a calm and considered manner. Fortunately, because the course is intended for this type of person, there are several (6) students who fit the category settler, staying in their original or a similar setting, possibly moving sideways into a teaching assistant role.

Arianne is a representative settler. On leaving school she had various jobs: at British Home Stores, in a hosiery factory, office manager at Argos, and an accounts job in a department store. Possibly some of this instability arose from opting to live with a number of relatives in turn rather than remain at home when her mother found a new partner. She married, had a son, and missed him so much that she gave up her job and went to work in the day nursery that was caring for him. When he was old enough he moved to the local pre-school and she stayed in the day nursery until, as he was finishing, she got a job in the pre-school.

At this point in the interview Ariane demonstrates that she intended to be a stager: 'I always said that when [my son] left primary school, I would actually work again, get another – go on to do accounts or something'. However, she was prevented from moving on by a second pregnancy. Arianne found that she liked pre-school work, even though 'there was no way I'd ever envisaged going into childcare' and decided to stay. Her career transformation was not particularly smooth. She had gained work in a very traditional setting that was not even functioning as legally required by its charity status. The two supervisors acted as owner-managers and were possessive about knowledge. This provoked Arianne to sign up for the Diploma because 'they wouldn't share information at all' and she 'wanted to know how the whole thing worked'. I fully remember how Arianne and subsequent Diploma students from the setting persuaded the parents to form the legally obligatory committee, who then quietly edged out the old hands.

Arianne has considered her decision to continue in the childcare setting carefully. Gaining her Diploma qualification 'gave me the option to leave'. 'It made me realise that I had other options. I didn't have to stay.' Arianne still puts her family first and plans to retire early when her husband, who is older, does so. For this reason she is not prepared to undertake further training, deciding that she will nominate a colleague to do the foundation degree rather than do it herself. She is clear that she intends to remain in early years work until she retires and makes the point that although her daughter is now at secondary school she does not 'feel the need' to move on: 'I'm settled now'. Some time after the interview she does, however, contact me to let me know that she has changed jobs and now runs a different setting further away from home. The conditions are better, her status improved, but not to step-upper levels. Her asserter characteristics, developed at a not-very-affluent British comprehensive school, presumably underpin her managerial prowess. She had been bullied there for being an upper middle-class child who had recently arrived from abroad.

Switchers

Switchers also appear to have adopted a childcare career but, unlike settlers, they have previously experienced a different career path and are choosing to change direction: they have other viable options. Sometimes the student described a very definite career progression; sometimes she had undertaken significant prior training; sometimes she strongly identified with a particular career, eg 'I worked in the police force as a civilian'. Occasionally the duration of a particular type of work was relevant, eg 'Seven years of that [insurance in the City] is enough for most people'.

The typology of switcher is illustrated by Evelyn's story, to counteract the overall tendency to focus on the high achievers who are more articulate. Evelyn tells a story of struggle to get out of an abusive relationship and to find a new and more fruitful career for herself. I was first alerted to her situation by the intensity of her claim that she enrolled on the Diploma to improve her confidence. Her story was unveiled slowly and it was some way through the interview that I began to make sense of what really happened and why confidence was so important to her. Whether the confused chronology was a result of Evelyn's tendency, as an agoniser, to talk around topics; an assumption on her part that I already had the more general picture; or a reluctance to share details until we had redeveloped a rapport, is difficult to determine, and possibly pointless as all three reasons might well be relevant. Evelyn has undergone counselling, so she could retell her story without getting upset.

Following troubled schooldays, Evelyn had worked in a shop and as a waitress before marrying. She then trained as a care assistant in the community, a job she did for about ten years, continuing part-time after her first child was born. One of her main tasks was to help elderly people prepare for bed. She was severely shocked when she found a client dead in bed: 'You deal with it at the time but afterwards you think, ooh, you know, and you go at nights'. This episode seems to have prompted her later decision not to return to caring as an occupation. However, her working and personal life both entered a period of crisis, as her husband became increasingly guilty of 'unreasonable behaviour'. These circumstances led to 'the onset of depression through what was going on at home' and a 'nervous breakdown'.

Recovering, and living with her mother and two young children, Evelyn began to help in the pre-school as part of her plan 'to be me again, not his wife, the kid's mum'. She followed the traditional path of parent helper and committee member before being offered a job, supplementing her earnings with lunch-time supervision and undertaking voluntary work in school in the afternoons in addition to her paid pre-school mornings. She enrolled on the Diploma course and when a colleague left, she became joint playleader and also the special educational needs co-ordinator, organising the additional support for the children who needed it: an area in which she would like to specialise. Just as her life was settling down, the co-leader decided to leave and she found her replacement to be a difficult person, who 'would undermine me every single step of the way'. Evelyn could not cope with the situation and soon found she was back on antidepressants: 'I was sick every morning before I went to work, physically sick before I went to work'.

Fortunately Evelyn managed to get a job as a special needs support assistant in the local school and decided to 'walk away' from the pre-school. Evelyn is now working as a teaching assistant (TA), doing some one-to-one work and running a benchmark reading scheme for the school. She is to do the level 3 TA course and wants to continue working in school: 'I love being with children ... I find it fascinating that children just interpret things differently'. She has considered and rejected the idea of reverting to her caring career. I make the point that perhaps having been depressed she needed to get away from illness and ageing, and she agrees: 'Yes, so it was, you go into a spiral and think, Where can I go with this career-wise?'

Step-uppers

Step-uppers are people who have stayed in childcare or closely related fields but have made an identifiable leap into a better-paid job with an annual salary nearer to the national average and clearly defined terms and con-ditions, line management and career routes. Fiona has taken her childcare training and found an alternative but related career where she can use some of her knowledge but also earn far more than the usual pre-school salary. This typifies the category of step-upper.

Having struggled to find solutions for her own premature twins, Fiona's motivation is to help children with special educational needs. She tried to do voluntary work in the local school but was refused on ethical grounds, as two of the children there were hers. When her children were small, Fiona became a childminder and then, commencing work in a local pre-school, enrolled on the Diploma course. She had already taken a psychology A-level and half-way through the Diploma decided she would like to train as a paediatric nurse to work with premature babies and go 'right to the heart of the problem'.

> You get to a point when you just think enough's enough and it was time to change direction.

Realising that she was seriously committed to this decision I gave her a reading list and allowed her to submit the final assignment three months early. This exempted her from a two-year access course in addition to allowing her to apply for and start a nursing course the following September rather than delay a year. Fiona managed to enrol on the nursing degree because her work was at an appropriate academic level. She credits her facility in essay-writing and child-development knowledge to the Diploma course. She also claims to use her child-protection and working-with-parents skills in her new career.

> I've still got my paperwork. I've kept it because I will need it at some point ... I've been through it at certain points when I have needed to look up child development.

> We use working with parents too – I deal with parents all the time.

After three years, she graduated as a nurse and obtained a post in a neonatal intensive care unit. She talks at length about research connecting neonatal pain to diminished neural development and how she wants to explore ways of preventing or minimising such effects. If she chooses to work full-time, Fiona now has the capacity to earn a national average wage. She is already committed to continuing with nursing: 'I shall be staying where I am', and delighted that: 'It's all come together now'.

> I didn't feel I was achieving my full potential. I feel like I have now, I feel content and like I've done it.

In her continual efforts to work with children with special needs, her decision to jump ahead and finish the Diploma early, and her determination to ensure that her own children achieve, Fiona demonstrates characteristics of an asserter, but one who supports others rather than manipulating them. Several times in the interview she talks about this:

> I wanted to help. I knew I wanted to help children with learning difficulties.

> I was able to help the other students. I then went on to teach what you had taught me. I went on to help others.

I told them all about spiral learning [cc, spiral curriculum] because ... all the students were sitting there going 'we've done this before'.

Attitudinal typologies

The students' dispositions are considered next. They reveal how attitudes mediate actions. On a continuum from *laissez-faire* to active intervention, *accepters* and *asserters* occupy polarised behavioural positions; *agonisers* alternate between action and self-doubt; while *accumulaters* systematically achieve new goals.

Accepters

Accepters project calm. They are neither striving to move forward nor worrying about direction, merely taking life as it comes. Some demonstrate greater agency than others, navigating a possible path to a possible goal, but without the sense of urgency or manipulation demonstrated by the asserters. Others react opportunistically to openings that arise. Some of the accepters' attitudes verge on the fatalistic, taking a path of minimum resistance, perhaps with a view to becoming more goal-oriented when their children are older and they have more time.

Amy typifies this category. She has a relaxed temperament and is capable of making choices but she is not particularly ambitious, and moves on only when nudged. She likes studying but is not motivated to seek promotion. Yet, ironically, she is one of the step-uppers in the study cohort who, when her children were more independent, moved into a 'properly paid' job. Before entering childcare, Amy had the potential to earn far more than her current (national average) salary, had she so wished. With a professional middle-class upbringing, and having attended a private Catholic primary school 'although we weren't Catholics', she passed the 11+ and went to an all-girls high school where she successfully passed O- and A-levels, before proceeding to university. She chose a four-year course offering a thorough grounding in all the academic disciplines. I initially construed this as demonstrating a liberal love of learning but later realised it could equally well represent a decision to delay specialisation and selection of a career path.

Amy met her husband early in her studies, married in her second year, and on graduating followed him to a northern city where, with an arts degree, she looked for work and found an unqualified post in a public library: 'I hadn't actually got a vocational degree or anything – so I wasn't quite sure what I wanted to do'. She worked there for five years, and when she had three children in quick succession, stopped work while they were small. The family moved house twice. When the youngest attended pre-school Amy moved effortlessly from committee member to paid worker: 'Yes I applied for it but people knew me, and things like that, and I'd been on the committee'. The work suited her and the family. She liked its flexibility and proximity to home: 'I didn't need to work for the money and I thought it was important to be at home while the children were little, um, and to be available for them really'.

Her decision to undertake the Diploma course was motivated by changes within the early years' environment: 'I can't remember exactly but legislation that said your staff had to have a qualification or something like that, and the committee encouraged us to do that, so that's how that came about'. That is not to say that she did not want to study: 'I mean, I enjoyed, liked the idea that I was furthering my knowledge about what I was doing' but she was not pro-actively seeking a qualification: 'I don't think there was any definite career plan behind it, no'.

When the existing leader retired, the four remaining staff decided to share the role of joint leader. Amy was one of the two qualified joint leaders so she could have made a bid for a greater share of the power. Instead, she continued sharing responsibility until a later 'group of mums' decided they would prefer to have a single leader and 'it all got quite nasty'. So Amy decided to look for work within a hospital environment and took a job three months later in an outpatients' playroom, as a preliminary step to training as a play specialist. This was an agentive decision but forced by circumstances.

> I would have maybe just drifted on at playgroup and in a way it was a good thing for me that it finished, it forced me to think. I think I probably come from a generation that thinks once you are in a job that's it, you are in it for life ...

Once qualified and in post, Amy appears content to continue with her current job. She is ambivalent about seeking promotion as she would no longer have contact with children, so did not apply when the co-ordinator post became vacant. Nor would she consider a move to gain promotion. This immobility is not a sign of low confidence, inflexibility or diminishing interest in her job – as she talks about plans to vary the work within her current role with enthusiasm – but merely an indicator of her satisfaction or *acceptance* of the status quo until it changes. She can afford to sit back and see what happens next.

Agonisers
Agonisers are an intermediate category of students who may display characteristics of either accepters or asserters as they swing from one view-point to another in an attempt to make and, retrospectively, to justify de-

cisions. There is an element of instability in their decision-making processes that for some may be quite inhibiting but for others may permit a degree of lateral thinking, even streaks of genius at times. The term is not intended to have critical connotations but to convey complexity. Agonisers think deeply about issues, are very self-reflective, and concerned to understand the significance of their own actions and those of other people. Agonisers vary with regard to how well they can resolve issues and move forward.

Frances admits openly: 'I do analyse myself ever such a lot'. Even her language demonstrated agonising: she used words like 'muddle' and 'messiness' throughout her interview. At the outset she surprised me by claiming that doing the Diploma was 'what made me stop going to playgroup'. Questioning revealed that 'I wasn't really having the right effect on those children'. Although she had worked happily in the group for six years before training, she decided that she had been 'just playing with the children' rather than educating them. The picture is more complicated, however, for Frances considers herself 'very admin based' and certainly her earlier career as a legal secretary and her later attempt to develop a policy package for use in after-school clubs support her claim. It is as if she can be organised on paper or completely unstructured when playing with children but not combine the two or modify either.

Frances did not want to be in charge: 'I don't know if I could have come up with the whole picture of what we should have been doing'. She uses a visual metaphor to explain her confusion: 'It's like being in the middle of a spider-graph, isn't it, and thinking, I don't know which leg to take'. She is very uncertain about responsibility, preferring a supportive role to a leadership one in her earlier career, in the pre-school and in her current job as arts co-ordinator in a secondary school. 'I don't need to be the peacock particularly, I'm quite happy to be the little peahen.' Her administrative role in the secondary school occasionally allows her to work with a group or with individual children and she admits to preferring to work with older children with whom one can converse more easily. 'Maybe the young age was too young so I couldn't really get the feedback maybe I needed from them.'

There are probably other issues, however. Co-considering her frequent references to muddle and mess, and her problems with assignments, I eventually recognise an underdeveloped ability to synthesise material. For Frances, an ordered and tidy physical environment allows her to focus. As she says: 'if it was like too messy, it messes my head'. Initially, I was sidetracked by her enjoyment of working 'creatively' with children, but on further questioning I discovered that 'practically' might be a better descriptor. Frances likes things to 'have a start and finish' and likes a 'product at the end'. Her practical hobbies include cake decorating and doing manicures: both tasks that need attention to detail, care, and an ability to work on a small scale. From this new understanding I began to see that one of the problems with the childcare course was that we advocate large-scale exploration of the media for small children, not adult-led craft. Therefore, the Diploma probably failed to value the type of 'creative' work that had attracted Frances into pre-school, and she is honest enough to admit this.

> It's funny that you should mention the mess because it's the one thing that — although I don't mind — I love children playing with it — their hands are filthy — playing with paint. I really like all that but in a controlled way.

Frances truly cares about children and could not accept any claims on her time that meant she could not give them her undivided attention. She explains how they are:

> little people that are going to grow up into big people and if you're feeling that in any way you are brushing them aside because you've got to go and fill out a form or do a bit of paperwork, that's dreadful.

Despite her inner stress, Frances was loath to move on: 'I liked the feeling of the ... little community playgroup so then the business thing of it clashed with me'. She did not move on cleanly. For a time she was working mornings in the pre-school, rushing into town to work afternoons as an insurance clerk, then at 5pm going to help at the after-school club. After four months she got the college job and gave up the pre-school and the clerking after a while but she ran the after-school club for a full year. Presumably there was some agonising about when and what to give up. Being a stager does not simplify this process.

Accumulaters

Accumulaters, in contrast, systematically collect qualifications or improve their job prospects without too much agonising. They are often lifelong learners and their chosen pathways may be eclectic or structured depending upon inclination, motivation and the opportunities presented. This category represents the entire spectrum of learners from the less able who dutifully collect basic qualifications: GCSEs and perhaps a selection of short course attendance certificates (eg Aileen), to those who cannot stop studying (eg Avril).

The categories relate to students' approaches to career and studying, not to any hidden personal crises. For instance, I categorise Holly as an accumulater as she demonstrates a straightforward approach to learning. Within her childcare career she is actively collecting every possible certificate. She has recently attained teaching assistant (TA) levels 2 and 3 and plans to do level 4, also a range of short specialist courses. Holly is ensuring that: 'should I want to move on and get a better wage, which I deserve, I will be able to do it'. Without the remainder of her narrative interview we would be unaware of the challenges she faces. A vicious attack left her agoraphobic and she struggles every day to overcome the problems this causes. But this is not the basis for the classification. She is not an agoniser in the sense that I define the category, because she is very forward-looking and employs strategies that enable her to achieve her chosen goals. If anything, she displays some asserter tendencies at times and perhaps this is why she is able to maintain a positive outlook.

Avril presents typical accumulater characteristics. Despite doing the 'basic minimum that I had to to get through' in compulsory education, she is now a lifelong learner collecting qualifications whenever possible. After having children and volunteering in the local pre-school, Avril switched careers from bookkeeping. Although she does not mention it at the interview, I remember that when Avril enrolled on the Diploma course she was still completing the introductory play course with me at an evening class. She was the only student to have requested permission to study the two courses concurrently rather than wait a full year to enrol on the Diploma. This simultaneous studying is something she has achieved for a second time, demonstrating her ability to focus and a commitment to study beyond the norm.

> I think I was actually finishing off my level 4 when I started to do my 7302 [teaching qualification] so I had a crossover of two courses at that point and I did actually have a timetable showing where I would fit everything in.

She is clear that it was the Diploma that whetted her appetite for study and for career progression. 'It was almost the courses shaping my career rather than me having a particular career in mind and doing the course through them.'

Certainly Avril has found the study habit. During the decade after obtaining her Diploma, she has also achieved an Advanced Diploma in Childcare (level 4), an Open Maths course, and the two stages of the post-compulsory teaching qualification (the 7302 and the Certificate in Education). It is the quantity and centrality of qualification-collection that justifies the category of accumulater. Avril applies the language of compulsion and programming when talking about her studies: 'addictive' 'habit' and 'study mode'.

> I think it can be quite addictive ... you kind of think 'well, okay, I've done that, I'm in the habit now' ... It's like your confidence is lifted and you are in the study mode so to speak and so you look for something else to do ...

Her entire interview focuses on educational issues and she demonstrates an ongoing interest and continual concern for pedagogic matters, talking at length about methods, standards and expectations within adult education. Unlike other students, she rarely strays into the personal, occasionally mentioning her children but only in an educational context. For Avril the educational is the personal. She displays accumulater characteristics when she explains how she moves from one area to another to keep a range of study areas active.

> I then had to divert over into getting my teaching qualification, and I got that and then I did a couple of things like basic skills to help me with my teaching so I'm only just now swapping over to the other route to do my vocational knowledge.

Avril also demonstrates how important confidence is and how easily it can be destroyed. She wants to achieve full-degree status and already has the forms to accredit her level 4 with the Open University. But a negative experience when completing the research element of her teaching qualification has made her doubt her abilities.

> Worrying with a degree because there will be more research ... When I done my Cert. Ed. I had a bit of trouble getting it the way that they wanted it ... I don't know whether I could do it at a higher level ...

Nevertheless, she recognises that a degree is the next step for her: 'I've got to go and do this degree'. So it is likely that her other wish, to do something for herself, like languages, will be deferred for a long while. As Avril specifically states: 'Education for myself is a way of life'. She is a definite accumulater, and also a step-upper.

Asserters

Asserters are goal-oriented. Most are determined to 'get on' and have taken every opportunity to do so. This manifests in different ways: proactively seeking the next promotion, challenging authority, or sometimes manipulating circumstances to bypass people standing in their way. Overall, there is a sense of unfulfilled ambition and a determination to shape their surroundings to create new opportunities. Successful asserters are highly motivated. They measure themselves against other people and use the information for personal betterment. They make childcare work for *them*, plan ahead and carve out career moves, rather than waiting for opportunities to arise. In defining this category I am concerned not with outcomes in terms of pay and job status but with the processes by which the individuals determine their own career paths.

Bella is a true asserter. She reports a childhood desire to escape her working-class origins, manifesting as a demand to stay on into the sixth form so that she could work in a bank, a career she equated with 'dressing up smartly to go to work'. She openly asserts her right to agency.

> I've always been quite firm about being independent ... you are the one that has got to live the life that you are setting yourself.

On leaving school Bella was immediately offered work in an estate agent's and enjoyed the sociability. Her parents insisted she accept a subsequent offer of work in a bank but, finding this uncongenial, she assertively changed occupation after only two weeks.

> I went into the estate agent's and I said to one of the guys there 'could you pretend to be my Dad and ring the manager at the bank and say to him that I am not coming back in?'

Presenting her parents with a *fait accompli*, she continued to sell properties, earning the position of office manager, but became dissatisfied when she recognised that only professionals could rise beyond that status.

> But then I came into contact with solicitors and surveyors and, um, people that had a different sort of education to me ... I could see how that changed your life and the level that you could live at.

This glass ceiling made the idea of returning to the job after having a family less attractive to her.

> I don't like being the pleb, I don't like being the new one. I like being quite bossy but knowing what I do. I don't mind going through the ranks as long as I can see a quick progression.

Bella found she genuinely liked looking after young children. As her own two children joined toddler and pre-school she displayed minor asserter tendencies, overcoming shyness to find the 'courage one day to poke my head round the door' and offer to help. She became a part-time assistant and was asked to enrol on the Diploma course but found that the pre-school supervisor, who was unqualified and very conservative, often blocked her initiatives. The threat of reduced hours when numbers were low was cause for concern, as her husband's business had closed. Bella tackled the situation by appealing directly to the committee. She convinced them that as she was the staff member undergoing training, a decision to cut her hours made no sense. Thus she learned that she could circumvent her supervisor's authority by appealing to the committee and she used this power quite flagrantly thereafter, undermining the supervisor, whom she saw as 'kind of sponging off me'.

In her next post she worked smoothly alongside the owner-manager for a time and was invited to open up independent afternoon-care in the same premises when she considered leaving. Bella even challenged Ofsted, finding a loophole in the regulations that allowed children to go straight from the morning to the afternoon session without the need to reclassify from sessional to full-day care. Inviting Ofsted to 'come and talk to me about it and I'll tell you how it is going to work' is certainly asserter behaviour. Problems arose when Bella sent a letter to parents offering them additional sessions. She claims to have discussed this with the owner: 'I thought that conversation had already happened', but the owner's reaction – she 'went absolutely *mad*' – implies a failure to communicate fully. Unabashed, Bella decides it is time to move on and is offered the post of headteacher of a local private nursery school. Her approach demonstrates an asserter attitude. On her application form she claims to have written:

> Please don't disregard me for the fact that I haven't got a teacher qualification because, you know, I am so passionate about what I do.

At the interview the panel commented: 'we couldn't believe just how enthusiastic you were'. However, people working under her sometimes found her very demanding. She describes how hurt she was when a colleague complained 'we've all got lives' and insisted 'you've got to realise... probably no one will do it to the level that you do it'. Whether she will achieve her aim of confining work to the workplace and 'having proper family time' is debatable but she is delighted to be 'escaping from the little back streets', and will command a salary two-and-a-half times her previous income, so she will be earning the title step-upper.

Taking an overview

In this chapter, we saw that, at the micro-level, the student group is not homogenous even though the majority are white British, married and with children. This leads me to question the validity of sorting respondents by sociological attributes and assuming further commonality, as is customary when qualitative research is extrapolated to large-scale survey data. However, an examination of patterns of living and working across the sample revealed that there are other characteristics that could be used to group students, leading to the two separate typologies, covering occupational relationships to childcare, and a broader range of attitudinal traits. Although an idiosyncratic classification, it does enable us to make comparisons across otherwise disparate data. The typologies identify distinctive groupings, suggesting that policy-makers may need to offer a range of incentives to encourage diverse workers to remain and progress in the profession.

Within the sample, the most common categories were switchers, accepters and agonisers (see appendix). Often switchers were either accepters or agonisers, demonstrating that most of the women changed career to work in childcare and that they tended to be either relaxed personalities or unsure about their personal ambitions; perhaps partly bearing out Skeggs' comments about the abnegation of self. Asserters tended to be settlers, switchers or step-uppers but never samplers or stagers, thus demonstrating stability in their goal-orientation. Accumulaters were never categorised as samplers, and no agoniser achieved step-upper status: all findings that support the internal logic of the typologies even with such a small sample.

Generally, the spread of attributions across the cohorts appears random but the step-uppers tended to group in the earlier six cohorts, samplers in the later three groups. It is likely that step-uppers need time to consolidate their achievements and find a progression route. This leads me to speculate whether, over time, samplers will find ways to use their childcare knowledge to open up new careers. Like many women before them, they may find a need to build on the skills and qualifications they already possess, regardless of their inclinations. In Sen's (eg 1999) terminology, they would be making choices from within their *capability sets*, a process of turning *capabilities* into *functionings* that Sen terms *conversion* (see chapter 4, cc).

With the typologies I am beginning the process of exploring how people's experiences are cumulatively significant. Childcare workers reading this book may want to pause here and think about their own trajectories. We know that life options are constrained by initial advantages, prior achievements and subsequent qualifications, but we have also seen how the outcomes for students making career choices within a range of co-realisable options can be significantly affected by human agency. On comparison, there is little evidence that the two sets of typologies are directly associated (see appendix), suggesting that individuals can turn their own lives around if they have determination and learn to use the qualities they possess. Even on superficial analysis, the differing degrees of energy required for step-uppers to self-improve is clear. The efforts of the accepter (Amy), the accumulater (Avril), and the asserter (Bella), vary in inverse relation to their familial and educational backgrounds, but all three are ultimately successful.

The students' narratives around which this chapter is constructed were chosen purely to demonstrate the two typologies and the process through which they were created. Nevertheless, a close reading of these accounts reveals the presence of characteristic behaviours that will be seen as significant in later chapters. None of the students had a definite career plan at the outset and two (Amy and Greta) admit to drifting into the work and (in Greta's case) out of it again when it proved less than satisfactory. Two (Arianne and Diane) express a desire to merge work and family commitments and one (Frances) talks of the 'sense of community' such work provides. Financial remuneration, the usual reward for work, plays a minor part in their decision-making: a 'bonus' (Fiona), and a key factor only when a partner's redundancy enforces this (Diane). Voluntary work appears in some cases to be equally important. Evelyn divides her time between paid and unpaid work, and Fiona considers a new career only when her plans to volunteer are thwarted on ethical grounds. Even the two step-uppers (Avril and Bella), who actively pursue careers in childcare, do this piecemeal. Avril collects qualifications and lets these 'shape' her career. Bella manipulates the environment to facilitate a staged self-advancement.

Overall, this chapter highlights the complex nature of life. We have a group of students with demonstrably different attitudes and work patterns who all gravitate towards work in childcare but with no clear career path in mind. There is clearly little observable connection between attitude and occupation: real life is more complex. This lack of clear association raises concerns about the efficacy of designing educational programmes to meet narrow instrumental objectives when more holistic gains are possible. The Diploma is a vocational course designed to meet the threshold standards for childcare work but the variations in student understanding and achievement and in the purposes to which they put their learning are considerable. This is evident in the individual narratives discussed in this chapter and becomes still more so as the student stories continue. Vocational learning can encompass far more than workplace knowledge: this pattern of integration could be replicated elsewhere.

At a practical level, holistic analysis is important, for it creates understandings that remain invisible when data is fragmented. The next chapter also takes a holistic approach. It shows that the strands in the women's lives are tightly interwoven and only an *integrated* framework can make sense of the way they organise their lives and the choices they make.

4

Making choices in real life

Making sense of complex data is a challenging process. We saw in the previous chapter how a holistic analysis draws attention to patterns across the narratives that ultimately become two typologies. Learning from this initial engagement how to make sense of the research material, I discarded analytical approaches that sought to dissect and code the interview material. Instead I chose further immersion in the interview transcripts, slowly feeling for the overarching patterns that could make sense of chaotic real-life relationships. As I began to analyse the transcripts, it became apparent that I could not and should not isolate the students' comments on education from their narratives about family and work. These subjects were closely linked and, after a while, I realised that this was significant. The students were positively motivated to integrate their lives, and the interview evidence demonstrated how they achieved this by making choices that *could* co-exist, establishing a network of reciprocal links that enabled the women to study, work and care for their families: all activities which required significant commitment, energy and time.

I had been slow to identify this pattern because earlier research into adult learning has a higher education focus and finds that adult women return to education in order to 'move on' in their lives. In the accounts of Rosalind Edwards (1993), Gillian Pascall and Roger Cox (1993) and Barbara Merrill (1999), education has a transformative function, helping women to move beyond the domestic sphere. Janet Parr's study (2000) shows that many women are overcoming traumatic events in their lives, seeking a fresh start.

However, the notion once formulated that the childcare students were seeking to integrate rather than change their lives is credible and the possible links through education easy to trace. Childcare knowledge is relevant to bringing up one's own children, and the vocational nature of the course draws the workplace into the net, lodging the student within a contextual framework that includes family, work and education. Later we see how the student personally relates to each of the contexts and consider the overarching connections between them, examining how they form a secondary set of links that further binds each student into a schema where family, education and work are vitally important and co-exist symbiotically.

The following chapters explore the wealth of detail that led to the construction of the integrated lives triangle, but here we examine the theory in abstract. Ironically, the triangle became visible because it explained a number of unexpected findings. I was surprised to learn that the students were content with their work despite its low-paid, part-time status. I was surprised that they were prepared to work as hard as they did for so little financial reward and that the boundaries between their paid and voluntary commitments were so poorly drawn and enforced. I was surprised, too, that their energies were so clearly focused on current activities, seeking through studying to balance their existing lifestyles rather than to improve their status. The students *did* plan for the future but with evident patience, waiting for the time to be right for change rather than actively shaping the future. Even the step-uppers, the accumulaters and the asserters were working within current structures rather than seeking radical change. For the women who were parents, their children's needs were a priority when planning work and study commitments, thus creating a triangular framework to bound their life choices.

Integrated lives theory

This *integrated lives* framework can be represented diagrammatically as a series of three interlocking triangles (see figure 1) and the reciprocal links described in generalised terms. On the outer framework, the childcare focus of the Diploma (representing education) includes content that supports the family as the student learns about child development theory and about education. Reciprocally, the student's practical knowledge of children assists assimilation of theory. Education, being vocational, directly increases the knowledge and competence the student takes into the workplace. Reciprocally, working in childcare extends and consolidates learning through practical experience. To complete the triangle, the family supports the workplace by allowing the students to have fuzzy life-work boundaries and put in additional unpaid efforts, whether to carry out planning and publicity, to fundraise or to provide the materials necessary for the children's activities. Reciprocally, the workplace offers convenient hours and location, and a sense of belonging to a community.

Figure 1 The triple triangle maintaining integrated lives © Hazel Wright, 2009

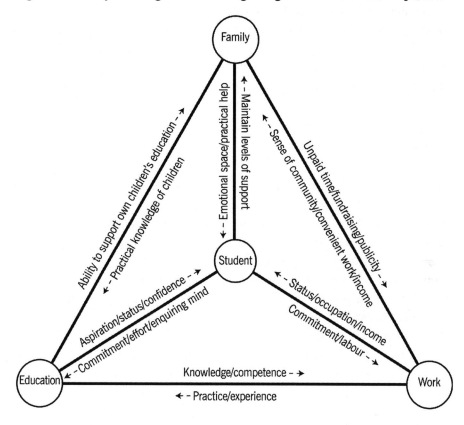

In the inner framework, the student supports her own family, foregrounding their needs at every stage and minimising the disturbance to their lives. Reciprocally, the family offers some practical help and the emotional space to study. From the workplace the student derives status, occupation and income without having to give up caring for her own family. Reciprocally, she offers labour and commitment and, in many cases, performs tasks over and above those that carry remuneration. This is an important aspect for pre-schools in the voluntary sector, as it is so financially constrained. From education the student gains status, confidence and a qualification and also new aspirations for the future. Reciprocally, the successful student makes a commitment to the course and college, demonstrating a desire to learn, an enquiring mind and a readiness to study – however difficult it is to find the time.

In seeking such a tidy theoretical explanation we should not forget that the real world is essentially 'messy'. In practice, there are many additional links across the boundaries. In real life, the women are juggling competing needs so the triangle represents a series of foci for compromise and negotiation rather than the idealised reflexively supportive nodes portrayed here. Nevertheless, the childcare student seeking to 'integrate life' is making choices which are clearly bounded by a triangle of interlinked contexts. For most women in this study, the family element is nuclear, comprising husband, wife and one or more children and this adds an additional layer of connectivity, further stabilising the structure within which they make their choices.

Biesta and Tedder (2007), analysing agency in adult education, assert that maintaining stability requires considerable energy in modern society when the pace of life is rapid and changing. This has parallels in the effort the childcare students put into integrating their lives, whilst, paradoxically, appearing also to 'drift' into childcare just because it is possible. The students work to provide a secure environment in which to bring up their children (family) and do so without sacrificing their own needs for a modicum of financial independence (work) and an element of personal improvement (education). That one or just a few women achieve this balance could be attributed to percipience, assertiveness or exceptional strength of character, but for so many to do so suggests the existence of supportive mechanisms. Looking across a range of disciplines, there are a number of different theories that collectively provide a social and psychological framework underpinning 'integrated lives'. The capability approach forms an external superstructure; so integrated lives theory occupies a localised space between underpinning and overarching theory. This hierarchy of structures is to be expected, as the capability framework is left deliberately 'incomplete' (Qizilbash, 2008:62) in the expectation that every user will customise it. As Sen states 'the capability approach is consistent and combinable with several different substantive theories' (1993:48).

Greedy institutions

To interpret the balance within the triangle I am drawn to Coser's (1974) theory of greedy institutions (cc). Initially applied to the concept of family by Coser and his wife, this was extended to include education by Edwards (1993, citing Ackers, 1980), and to childcare work through my research. A greedy institution is one that seeks total commitment from its members, and within the public sphere – the predominately male domain – its demands are normatively curbed through legislation or other official action. Hours of work, for instance, are normally legally restricted in the public sphere, offering people some protection.

Unchecked, however, a greedy institution is 'omnivorous'. It seeks 'voluntary compliance', finding 'means of activating loyalty and commitment' through 'appearing highly desirable to the participants' (Coser, 1974:6). This state-ment underscores the vulnerability of women, functioning in the private sphere and juggling part-time roles that so often define their sense of belong-ing and self-esteem. The family and domestic tasks demand constant atten-tion, education requires open-ended personal study time, and childcare work exacts an emotional commitment that cannot be measured in terms of hours or effort. Within my research, the voluntary status of the settings and the part-time nature of both study and work make it even more difficult to define or restrict ways of complying. We find that the women welcome fuzzy life-work boundaries for the flexibility they offer in terms of reducing hours away from the home. The practice of studying in spare moments when it does not dis-turb the family also exemplifies an activity with poorly defined boundaries.

In her interview, Heena unwittingly draws attention to the greedy status of all three institutions. With regard to her family commitments she claims to 'run around like a loon'. She likes assessment criteria in education as they set boundaries. Her concern is 'where do you stop?' In the workplace she des-cribes how the required commitment 'builds up, builds up, builds up until it's too much'. Yet her husband is 'supportive of me'. He joins the pre-school com-mittee, he takes her to college in advance to help her cope with agoraphobia, he changes his work schedule to facilitate course attendance, but he does *not* do the housework. Heena's outlook is positive, connecting family, work and education: 'it's good for my kids to see me working and studying'.

The concept of greedy institution may also explain why, acting intuitively, some women conceal their studies, marginalising education within the home. Coser believes that different 'status positions' are possible when an indivi-dual's behaviour is 'not observable by all his role-partners or status-partners at the same time' (*ibid*:7). Given that husbands know, or think they know, what is happening on the home front, and given that many already see their wives as working too hard for too little pay, concealing the extent of their educational commitment may be the only action open to the women.

Thus the women's engagement with, and enjoyment of, their family, work and study inheres greedy institution status to all three aspects of the triangle. Students live within the reciprocal triangle, exhibiting varying degrees of con-sciousness of its existence, and work to maintain the balance between the contexts. At one level the very flexibility that the women value makes them vulnerable. At another, the integrated triangle is self-checking and, therefore, inherently stable. In effect, each pair of greedy institutions checks the dominance of the third, keeping the system in stasis. Later we shall see how additional commitments are accepted until they impinge too greatly on another element, and at this point the students – or their partners – complain. The balance is then redressed, so the overall stability of the integrated lives is maintained and within it the freedom to choose. Greedy institutions have to be either tolerated or tamed and the integrated lives triangle may serve as a taming influence.

In general, the students were content with the choices they made rather than striving for more. Some complained about factors like poor pay and working conditions but this did not motivate them to move on. Most enjoyed studying and accepted the need to do it in their spare time. Not one indicated the slightest desire for her children to grow up and become independent, so she was free to progress to the next stage of her life. This demonstrated the central importance of the family for these women. It was precisely this sense of fulfilment that first suggested the notion of integration, of choices made willingly. However, the high degree of personal satisfaction I observed led me to consider its validity further, to question whether their expectations were in some way curtailed.

Cognitive dissonance

From within psychology the concept of cognitive dissonance (cc) has some relevance to this study. This general notion can be attributed to many acceptable decisions. Festinger (1957) found that people who hold contradictory attitudes will strive to reduce tension by changing one attitude to fit the other. Women who choose to work in childcare might well be trying to fulfil the role of mother and also work without encountering dissonance. When Fiona talks of returning briefly to her previous occupation and deciding 'I couldn't cope with work' and 'that's when I went into childcare', she appears to be implying that the two are qualitatively different – that childcare work is the more acceptable proposition, possibly not even considered to be work. However, as convenience and manageable hours are very important in their own right, this could be purely a practical matter. Overall, it seems the women want to be with their children and are exercising choice in the context of the family. Faye is typical when she states: 'I knew that I had to do something that involved ... around school or university so that I could have ... the time off with them'.

Adaptive preference

Returning to the issue of curtailed expectations, the psychological concept of adaptive preference (cc) is repeatedly discussed in connection with the capability approach and partially equates to Sen's (1999) term *mental conditioning*. Economists use the term 'preference' to mean choice; for psychologists the term 'adaptive' refers to an animal or person adjusting to fit their environment. Therefore *adaptive preference* implies that an individual is altering his or her needs to fit with what is seen to be possible, accepting a set of reduced options as normal. The question therefore arises of whether the women are truly content or whether they are so conditioned to meet the demands of family life that they unconsciously accept that the needs of partners and children are more important than their own, and, so to speak, 'cut their cloth accordingly'.

Examining the student narratives in detail reveals that the women make their choices knowingly. When they put other people's needs before their own they do so either to keep the peace or out of altruism, not because they know no better, suggesting that their preferences are not adaptive even though they align with common cultural norms. This fits with Jonathan Elster's work of 1982 on adaptive preference. He analyses the concept and identifies five distinctive qualities that equate with adaptive preference formation. For brevity, I refer to them as: reversibility, choice restriction, endogeneity, optionality and reactivity.

Reversibility implies that choices would change if conditions were modified and that they are therefore not freely made. There is possibly an element of this in the decision of stagers to work in childcare when their children were little but not to remain in the profession. However, most interviewees, even if moving on, were enthusiastic about their time in the field, so their decision can be seen as opportunistic rather than adaptive. *Choice restriction* would indicate that women choose childcare because their options are limited but we shall see that the evidence refutes this: many who choose to work in childcare do so because they want to, not from lack of alternatives. Indeed, several students point out that they could earn more money for less effort if they worked in a supermarket.

Endogeneity relates to whether choices are genuine or falsely induced and it appears that the women chose childcare work rather than being coerced into it. Later chapters confirm this. *Optionality* again refers to the nature of choice, this time asking whether the chooser consciously makes a choice or is driven compulsively towards a particular option, so touching on biological conditioning (ie whether maternal urges compel women to care for children). This does not appear to be the case (see discussion later in the chapter and section on maternal identity in chapter 5).

Finally, *reactivity* implies that choices are made to fit a particularly impelling option but this narrowing of choice is denied retrospectively through a form of false justification. This usually becomes apparent when options expand. If decisions are reactive, people cling to them inappropriately and cannot take advantage of a broader array of choice. The forceful protests of a few students in the face of change (in particular Celia and Frieda) possibly indicate an element of *reactivity*. Both seemed to advocate greater professionalisation of the workforce but also appeared to be threatened by policies that bring childcare work more in line with the external world. However, the evidence overall suggests that the students are openly choosing their employment (discounting *restricted choice*), are genuinely wanting to work with children rather than being coerced (discounting *endogeneity*), or instinctively driven to do this (no lack of *optionality*) so the degree of adaptation is minimal.

This brief discussion of adaptive preference concludes that the students are freely choosing their options even though the array is prescribed by their role in, and commitments to, the family. There may be a small element of adaptive preference – instances are identified within the text – but generally caring for children, one's own and other people's, appears to be an elective decision and the students conscious of the choices they are making. Accumulaters demonstrate a realistic awareness of what they can achieve one step at a time. Asserters reveal a high degree of self- and other-awareness as they take advantage of opportunities that arise. Agonisers may not easily find a direction but they demonstrate an ability to see both sides of an argument. Accepters may only make decisions reactively but when they do so appear to recognise that they have exercised choice. So it is more accurate to talk about contingent selection rather than adaptive preference. Students make choices that suit them *now* and defer other choices until they become viable. Looking ahead to the discussion of capability later in this chapter: to view the students' decisions in terms of selecting achievable functionings from their current capability set is more flexible and sensitive to individual circumstances, and allows the possibility of change as capabilities expand.

Reacting to social expectations

Given the students' maturity and their acceptance of traditional family values, earlier literature that ascribes guilt and anxiety to separation from one's own children is relevant – also the coercive nature of political influence. We must consider the possibility that the women's actions are conditioned by values which were inculcated earlier (which would be a form of adaptive preference).

> Societies go through phases of wanting their mothers to be at home with their children, and find many ways of pressurising the women into whatever is deemed socially desirable. (Price, 1988:89)

Moves towards gender equality in society may have been overstated. Carol Vincent summarised this view in 2000 (pp26,27). She cites Diane Reay's (1998) claim that the term *parental* 'glosses over maternal responsibility' and suggests that involvement of fathers is not always equal in reality. She also restates Miriam David's (1993) argument that maternal employment has increased the responsibilities inherent in motherhood. Vincent reminds us of evidence from Brannan and Moss (1991) that even in 'dual earner households' responsibility for providing or finding childcare falls predominately on the mother. However, the women have a role in these matters – the students described in this book are *choosing* to balance their multiple commitments, are taking most of the responsibility for their children and clearly exhibiting *agentive* behaviour. They are exercising the choice to care for their own children in the face of current political agendas that favour the expansion of paid childcare and women returning to the workforce soon after having a child. As childcare trainees, they know that John Bowlby's views (1951) on maternal attachment are out of favour and that cross-cultural studies support multiple care-giving and therefore justify paid day care. They are aware that if they choose to look after their own children they are acting counter to current trends.

Working in childcare, as my research shows, is one way of dealing with 'maternal responsibility' whilst allowing the possibility of personal growth, and of meeting the expectation of contributing to the family income. It appears that the students are making choices from what Bernard Williams (1987:100) termed 'co-realisable capabilities'; in other words, from within their capability set (cc).

Supporting the community
My research indicates that, in addition to those who work in pre-school in order to care for their own children or to develop their employability, there are some who seek a sense of belonging in the community. This requires further theoretical exploration. The conceptualisation of integrated lives foregrounds family, workplace and educational setting as the main *loci* for social interaction and this is in keeping with the overall tenor of the interviews. But this is not the entire story. Family and work matters blend seamlessly into community concerns, a transition that is helped by the social nature of early years work, particularly in the voluntary sector. The Diploma course, being voca-

tionally oriented and having a focus on young children and their needs, creates an additional indirect link between education and the community. Theoretically, the connections to the wider community frame the integrated triangle, reinforcing the linkages and further increasing its stability. Perhaps, therefore, there is a case for enclosing the integrated triangle within a circle labelled community (figure 2). Certainly the evidence of community involvement suggests that social capital is relevant to the women's choices.

Social capital

The concept of social capital (cc) was first formulated by the French sociologist Pierre Bourdieu and significantly developed by, among others, economist James Coleman (1988:S119) who defined it as a combination of 'obligations and expectations, which depend on trustworthiness of the social environ-

Figure 2: Integrated lives strengthened by community ties

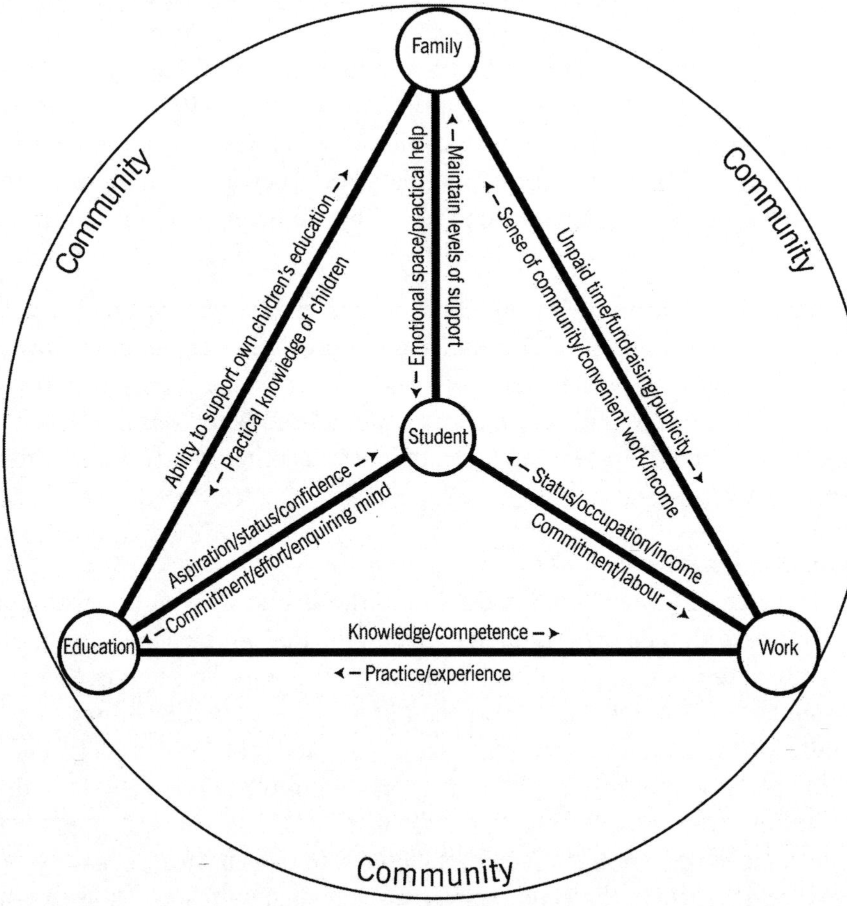

ment, information-flow capability of the social structure, and norms accompanied by sanctions'. In other words, it describes the give-and-take networks which exist between individuals and groups in society who trust each other and know that if they support other people the support will be reciprocated when they need help and that the social group will actively ensure that this happens. The term capital is used because these reciprocal networks can represent significant financial assets even though the transactions avoid monetary exchange. They may include exchanges with measurable value, as in the offer of free babysitting; or they may be more abstract, as in the sense of self-worth gained from being treated as a friend by someone you perceive to be important. The concept was popularised by Robert Putnam in his analysis of American society, *Bowling Alone* (2000) that studies positive social networks but also the negative effects of close-knit communities that manifest as sectarianism, bigotry and corruption. Thus social capital serves to capture the relational elements underpinning society and offers a supporting concept through which to filter the interpersonal consequences of education. These are quite distinct from the instrumental and economically orientated connections embedded in the human capital (cc) debate.

Community ties

The literature on both the benefits of education (see especially, Schuller *et al*, 2004) and social capital (particularly Putnam, 2000; Halpern, 2005; Baron, Field and Schuller, 2000) suggests the two are connected. So it could be expected that the students would be motivated to run voluntary organisations, enter local politics or join community groups, but this was not very evident. However, as with the exploration of integrated lives, adopting a deeper and more holistic approach made visible a fuller interpretation. Integration is fundamental to the social capital discussion. The community element of the students' lives is so embedded as to be almost invisible but comments about drifting into pre-school, working alongside their children, and being active on committees before being offered work all demonstrate a high level of community involvement, as do volunteering in school and caring for other peoples' children.

Community is embedded in the women's primary choices. Some students, notably Danni and Bethany, were very clear about the importance of community, particularly in relation to local schools, revealing altruistic and status reasons for staying in childcare. A minimal concern for rates of pay, and fuzzy boundaries between paid and unpaid work also suggest that the job is seen as an extension of community service. Evelyn's complaints about a colleague who 'expected to be paid for everything' illustrate the blurring of boundaries. Putnam (2000) devotes an entire chapter to altruism, volunteering and philanthropy all of which he identifies as vital elements in social capital formation. Therefore it is reasonable to deduce that the students were heavily involved in the development and maintenance of social capital within their local communities but achieved this through their family and workplace connections. Thus community networks are important but not of primary significance. They are actually mediated through other aspects of the integrated lives triangle, pointing again to the relevance of figure 2.

Friendship ties

Social capital theory also contributes to an explanation of the transient nature of friendships made on the Diploma course. Despite settling very quickly, and displaying a high level of congeniality within the classroom, few of the women made lasting friendships. They talked about 'life moving on' and being very busy people, but this does not fully explain how successive cohorts so easily lost touch when the course finished.

A study of social capital as a multi-level concept does, however, offer a possible explanation for this finding through the notions of bonding and bridging. Putnam uses the phrase *bonding* to explain the 'inward looking' connections between homogeneous groups of people. Conversely, *bridging* describes the formation of 'outward looking' links, encompassing people 'across diverse social cleavages'. Putnam refers to these as 'superglue' and 'WD-40', a well-known lubricant. Halpern and Putnam both believe that people who are high in one form of capital are high in the other too: those who already have close friendships and professional networks are more able to develop further associations. Thus, if we take a micro-level perspective, we view each woman as closely bonded to others in her local community through her involvement in the workplace. On enrolling on the Diploma, she represents her community in the wider sphere. She develops bridging networks with the other students, acting as a conduit for information and point of contact for interaction between the communities. This sense of connectedness can be seen in Felicity's comment: 'you get to feel more comfortable going into these courses because there always seem to be familiar faces' or Arianne's: 'I knew that I could pick up the phone to somebody ... I knew that somebody would be there'.

As bonding begets bridging, it makes theoretical sense that students enrolling on a childcare course and with a strong background in community involvement would rapidly form a supportive group ethos. It also makes sense that these ties may be short-lived for, as Halpern observes, bridging social capital decays much faster than bonding, supporting a view that in a situation where close community ties exist (strong bonding), new networks (bridging) may be of less long-term significance. Bourdieu himself (1997/86) believed that social capital needs to be continually worked at to endure. Together, these factors help to explain the rapid decline of course-based friendships once the course is over. So arguably, the tightness of the integrated triangle precludes a need to maintain other networks. Friendship, like community, lies outside the core triangle of family, workplace and classroom. Within the educational apex, it stays inside the course framework; a situation probably reinforced by the busy lives the women lead that make additional involvements difficult to maintain. Living within traditional family structures and working in local communities, the women have other ties that take precedence over new friendships, other issues that have priority when making choices.

Social meshing

The social capital debate tends to focus at meso- and macro-levels, justifying the notion that individualism is rife in contemporary society and we no longer collectively care for, or even consider, the needs of others: the story of 'social capital lost' (see Edwards, 2004). In their failure to engage at the level of family, conventional discussions of social capital miss both inequalities within the family and the processes operating at the micro-level where, as this study reveals, women in particular are actively creating and strengthening local ties. In chapter 7, the term *social meshing* is used to describe the co-hesive role of the Diploma: the women's activity is fine-grained, filling gaps in the social fabric rather than creating new frameworks. Rather than offering a conventional interpretation of social capital, this study captures the concept at micro-level.

However, as it foregrounds the importance of choice as well as recognising both individual needs and the relational contexts in which they are enmeshed, the capability approach offers a more appropriate conceptual framework, as detailed consideration of this approach illustrates.

Capability approach

The capability approach (CA) provides additional support for the students' choosing processes, since the triple triangle of integrated lives appears to define the boundaries of the childcare students' capability set. The harmony between the familial, vocational and educational contexts may arise because, in valuing integrated lives, the students are choosing co-realisable possibi-lities from within a gendered capability set, making decisions that keep the different elements in balance. The capability set describes the possibilities open to an individual. As part of this process it must clarify the connections between options. Some may be achievable in tandem, more of one permitting more of another. Some may be mutually incompatible, necessitating a choice between one and another. Others may require a compromise, more of one necessitating less of another. Each individual will have a unique capability set but in more general terms, groups of people with shared characteristics may have sets in common. I believe this is the case for the cohort of childcare workers. The integrated lives triangle represents their collective capability set, and stands as an empirical example of the capability approach activated. Later in the chapter we explore this connection to see how it expands the explanatory power of both triangle and CA.

First, we must familiarise ourselves with the capability approach. This framework was developed in the 1980s and 1990s by economist Amartya Sen (1985a, 1985b, 1987, 1992, 1995, 1999), sometimes in association with philosopher Martha Nussbaum (Nussbaum and Sen, 1993) who also worked on the theory independently, particularly in relation to women and development (1995 with Glover; 2000). It is a liberal ideology that recognises the diversity of individuals and upholds their right to make their own choices in life. It embraces the view that policies formulated to benefit the majority often perpetuate existing structural divisions in society, as those most able to access and utilise resources do so, thus excluding those that cannot. Sen believes that the right to choose should belong with citizens rather than external decision-makers. He believes that when we evaluate choices we should judge individuals' achievements in terms of their own values and objectives, whether or not we also use external criteria. Thus, the capability approach empowers people to live life in the way *they* want to.

To understand the capability approach it is necessary to consider what it stands against. Sen explains this himself in his classic work, *Development as Freedom* (1999). Traditionally, governments create policy to achieve 'optimum' outcomes, but these are often derived from unrealistic assumptions. Under Classical Utilitarianism (after Bentham, cc utilitarianism), policy offered a single option (preference) believed to best benefit the majority. Economists would total assumed preferences to identify an optimum choice, and, believing that people make rational choices, they thought the majority would themselves choose this option if given a choice. This notion relies on a number of hypothetical judgements; it is by no means assured that the optimum solution will suit everyone, nor that people will identify a particular option as the best. So, seeking a fairer method, Libertarians advocated policy based upon people's rights – but this treats individuals as similar units. Sen recognised that 'the effect of ignoring the interpersonal variations can, in fact, be deeply in-egalitarian' (1992:1), because it is what people can do with a resource, or its *conversion*, that matters – not the resource itself. For instance, a free parking space is of no use to someone who has no car!

Conversion relies on personalised information and even if this were publicly available it could not easily be aggregated. Even if it could be, aggregation by family and social groupings often disguises the disadvantage of some con-stituent members, particularly women and children, the elderly or unwell. Indeed, the poorer treatment of individuals in impoverished families may disappear from sight altogether in statistics focused on heads of households or family units. Because it challenges such inequalities, the capability ap-proach can be described as an 'ethically individualistic' philosophy (Robeyns, 2008) with an ultimate concern for the well-being of the individual. This is not to be confused with individualism as a selfish trait. It is quite different from the call for the 'individual to lead a life of his own beyond any ties to the family or other groups' of Beck-Gernsheim (2002:ix) and late modernism (cc indivi-dualisation). Nor does it refute the importance of relational ties or the ethics of care. Quite the opposite: it is concerned that we observe and act upon the hidden inequalities that lie within broader family groupings, to improve everyone's life-chances.

Sen's initial interest lay in development economics so his arguments are poli-tically orientated (eg development as freedom) and illustrated by examples from poorer societies. Nevertheless, his terminology and the underpinning concepts have a practical application beyond this specialist usage. We have learned that he describes the choices people make in terms of functionings (cc) and capabilities (cc), and I use Sen's definitions to describe functionings as 'the various things a person may value doing or being' (ie the options they choose to realise), and capability as 'the alternative combinations of func-tionings that are feasible for her to achieve' (ie the choices which are pos-sible). Thus *realised* functionings are 'what a person is *actually* able to do' and the capability set is 'her real opportunities' (1999:75), or 'potential'.

In policy terms, Sen sees capability formation as a new space for political intervention. If new initiatives support a broad range of options and *increase* capability, individuals can decide for themselves what they want to do, or in Sen's terminology, have a greater choice of functionings. Thus, individuals benefit from a greater sense of agency but also from selecting options that better meet their needs. Society benefits because resources are put to better use and people are more contented. In focusing upon *freedoms* rather than on basic resources (inputs) or outcomes (outputs) the capability approach recognises the complexity of real lives and the constraints within which many people live, anticipating the move away from the position that equality of opportunity is commensurate with treating everyone the same.

The capability approach also refutes the instrumentalism underpinning contemporary society, for Sen is concerned with people's satisfaction rather than with measurable outputs. His conception of the standard of living is essentially broader than economic necessity: he claims that 'commodities are no more than means to other ends' and that 'ultimately the focus has to be on what life we lead and what we can or cannot do, can or cannot be' (Sen, 1987: 16). Thus his work challenges current notions of performative measurement, since he favours uncertainty over simplistic statistical generalisation: 'Why must we reject being vaguely right in favour of being precisely wrong?' (1987: 34). Indeed Sen's whole approach not only advocates choice but in its flexibility and lack of specificity, enables choice. The CA is deliberately *incomplete* so as to allow people to determine their own values.

Taking advantage of this openness, I determined to use my empirical evidence to customise the capability approach, specifically the process of conversion as the transition from capability to functioning is central to making choices. The biographical nature of the student accounts supported an investigation of longer-term outcomes and how they were achieved when the occupational typologies were recast as indicators of functionings. Used statically as in chapter 3, they identify a student's current status, her degree of commitment to the profession at a point in time. However, they also have the potential to be used sequentially and to serve as a proxy for achievement. Over time, samplers could become stagers and settlers or switchers, and ultimately step-uppers if they continue to progress in a childcare or related career. This introduces a dynamic element into the analysis, and demonstrates its cumulative nature. In many cases a capability was developed and turned into a functioning and this then became an extended capability for further conversion, expanding the range of choice.

To demonstrate the cumulative nature of capability, we look again at Evelyn, whom we met as a switcher in chapter 3. She turned her potential to relate to people (a capability) into a skill and worked successfully as a social-carer (a functioning). A negative factor (an abusive husband) caused a second negative factor to develop (mental illness), temporarily reducing her capability. However, on recovering and taking up work in a pre-school (a new functioning), Evelyn acquired the capability to become a teaching assistant working with special needs children. This final functioning cumulatively converted the function of carer and the function of pre-school worker into the more specialised functioning of special needs assistant.

Thinking in such a mechanical fashion drew my attention to commonalities in the material, over and above the variety in the detail. When recounting their life stories, the students tended to mention the same factors: background characteristics, family support, schooling and, repeatedly, the importance of earlier educational experiences in determining their ability to achieve, their inclination to study further, and their confidence to return to education as adults. Despite their individuality there was a consistency to the subjects that arose in the interviews and I could hear in the tone of their voices and fluency of narration, how the students held those early situations or experiences accountable for future achievement or lack of it. Collectively, the students were identifying a number of variables that affected their choices.

Identifying capability indicators

It was fairly straightforward to turn the commonalities into a set of indicators representing the key elements of the life-course and then to identify levels within each indicator, to facilitate comparison between individuals. Table 2 overleaf offers six key indicators:

A class

B familial support

C experience within compulsory education

D level of current qualification

E job status (as a proxy for seniority and reward)

F health (an important absence for some).

This is only a preliminary analysis using a simple ranking system, so disguises significant distinctions, such as whether ill health was historic, current or chronic. There is no intention to create mathematical scales or seek causal connections or predictive capacity. The open nature of the data collection process makes this impossible.

For any individual student it is possible to produce a set of indicators (A to F) that represent different capabilities available at key points in their lives, and this allows us to make some comparisons between students and their specified functionings, the choices they could make.

Table 2: Capability indicators

Indicator	Range	Descriptive Label
A. Class [based on informal comments about family occupation, status, beliefs]	1-3	1. Manual 2. Clerical 3. Professional/managerial
B. Familial support	-1 +1	-1 Negative (including abusive) +1 Positive
C. Compulsory educational experience [adapted from Bernstein's instrumental and expressive 'means' and 'ends' (2003)]	1-5	1. Alienated (rejected education and its goals) 2. Estranged (accepted education, rejected goals) 3. Indifferent 4. Detached (rejected education, accepted goals) 5. Committed (accepted education and its goals)
D. Qualification level [using standard levels]	0-7	0. No qualifications 1. Entry level 2. O level/GSCE 3. A level 4. Degree yr 1 (certificate) 5. Degree yr 2 (diploma) 6. Degree yr 3 (honours) 7. Postgraduate
E. Job status [using categories chosen for questionnaire analysis]	1-5	1. Volunteer/unemployed 2. Assistant/non-professional 3. Supervisor/room leader 4. Deputy/manager 5. Senior manager
F. Health	-1 +1	-1 Negative +1 Positive
G. Attitudinal typology	1-4	1. Accepter 2. Agoniser 3. Accumulater 4. Asserter
H. Occupational typology	1-5	1. Sampler 2. Stager 3. Settler 4. Switcher 5. Step-upper

Included in the table but different in kind are the rankings for the attitudinal categories (G). These are used as proxies for agency, as they often serve a catalytic function, influencing the degree and pace of achievement rather than being indicators in themselves.

The occupational typologies (H), which in this analysis represent the outcomes or functionings, appear in the same table but represent summative outcomes rather than indicators.

Creating capability chains

We now have a list of indicators applicable to every student. Each indicator can be ranked (with minus values or 0 being the lowest) to give every student a unique set of codes which can be displayed quite simply as a linear, or capability, chain as below.

ID	A	B	C	D	E	F	G	H
	Class	Familial support	Compulsory educational experience	Qualification level	Job status	Health	Attitudinal typology	Occupational typology

The chains can also be converted to block diagrams to facilitate visual presentation, strengthening their immediate impact. This is simply a device for at-a-glance comparison of formative influences, to allow salient distinctions to stand out and to allow student data to be compared and contrasted without resorting to re-reading the narratives.

To give an example, see the capability chains overleaf for three step-uppers, Amy, Avril and Bella, respectively an accepter, an accumulater, and an asserter.

Amy

A1	A	B	C	D	E	F	G	H
	3	+1	5	6	5	+1	1	5
+6								
+5								
+4								
+3								
+2								
+1								
-1								

Avril

A1	A	B	C	D	E	F	G	H
	2	0	2	3	5	+1	3	5
+6								
+5								
+4								
+3								
+2								
+1								
-1								

Bella

A1	A	B	C	D	E	F	G	H
	1	0	5	3	5	+1	4	5
+6								
+5								
+4								
+3								
+2								
+1								
-1								

This device shows how the three step-uppers have in common only their final status and positive health. They started life differently advantaged, as they came from across the three social-class categories, but they all had neutral or positive childhoods.

Amy experienced the most supported childhood: she was upper middle class, actively encouraged by her parents, had a positive educational experience and was allowed to study to degree level (see chapter 3), opening up her choices. This pattern of relative prosperity and success perhaps explains her accepter stance; she had no need to strive to succeed but could wait to see what opportunities arose naturally.

Avril, in contrast, came from a lower middle-class background and was estranged at school (she concealed her academic potential to avoid being bullied). She gained some level 3 qualifications in the tertiary sector and de-cided later to try to make good her educational deficit and broaden her choices. Lacking a high level of family support at this stage, she enrolled on a series of courses until she slowly attained a level of qualification commen-surate with her abilities and developing aspirations. This again seems a logical pattern of behaviours for someone of her background, who was identified earlier as an accumulater. She needed to expand her choices step by step.

In comparison, Bella, who had a greater social distance to travel, resorted to actively manipulating the environment to make good her disadvantage, demonstrating distinctive asserter characteristics throughout her adult years. She told us (see chapter 3) that her parents were working class (section A) and unqualified and that she negotiated their agreement to an education to A-level but knew that to continue into higher education would be impossible. She talked about her enjoyment of school and recognises its instrumental value (so is classed as committed in section C) and has argued, earned and manipulated her way to a position of authority in the workplace. Her assertive behaviour compensated for initial limited choices.

The patterns of behaviour (or agency) adopted by each of these three stu-dents make perfect sense, when viewed alongside the other capabilities already in their sets.

Next I discuss the chains of the remaining two step-uppers (Felicity and Fiona, see overleaf) and examine the integrity of their accounts. It is then useful to compare their chains with that of Irma, a student who was not in a position to step up, and consider why Irma lacked this capability.

Felicity

A1	A	B	C	D	E	F	G	H
	3	+1	5	6	5	+1	1	5
+6								
+5								
+4								
+3								
+2								
+1								
-1								

Fiona

A1	A	B	C	D	E	F	G	H
	3	+1	5	6	5	+1	1	5
+6								
+5								
+4								
+3								
+2								
+1								
-1								

Irma

A1	A	B	C	D	E	F	G	H
	3	+1	5	6	5	+1	1	5
+6								
+5								
+4								
+3								
+2								
+1								
-1								

Felicity came from an advantaged background and was sent to a Catholic school. However, her level of family support is classed as neutral, as her mother both intervened in her education in the early stages and neglected to follow this up when it mattered during public examinations. Felicity enjoyed school but left with basic GCSEs. So we can see that she needed to overcome her earlier accepter stance and make considerable effort in the workplace (column E) in order to progress.

It is post-Diploma that Felicity has completed her education, opportunistically enrolling on the Foundation Degree, as she found she liked studying. She controlled her accepter tendencies and developed a second career. Quite possibly, her early advantages and enjoyment of school gave her the confidence to return to education: to a large extent the poor educational qualifications were a deviation from expectation rather than anticipated. If she continues as an accepter she may drift into new opportunities if they arise but there is also a danger that her achievements will plateau or even drop back if she is operating beyond her comfort levels in her new career.

Fiona, in contrast, came from a disadvantaged background (both working class and unsupportive) but, despite rarely attending, recognised the value of an education (a detached attitude to schooling) and struggled to achieve GCSEs and later a single A-level. She displayed pronounced asserter qualities to achieve this and a determination to enter nursing once she saw that the Diploma course gave her the necessary extra level 3 qualification. We can see from her chain that she has worked continually to overcome her earlier disadvantages.

Despite different strengths and weaknesses these students were all able to achieve because they had positive attributes to offset against negative and because differing agentive actions could compensate for lower initial capabilities. Their actions contrast with those of a lower achieving student like Irma, a stager and accepter.

The difference can be clearly seen when her chain is compared to theirs. Irma came from a working-class family and described her childhood as unhappy, providing evidence of a difficult relationship with her mother. Her description of her schooling paints her as rebellious and disaffected but she turned up regularly and claims to have had plenty of friends so I have classified her as estranged rather than alienated. She achieved six CSEs but left with no idea about what she wanted to do. Her early career resembled a sampler's, as she flitted from one low paid job to another. However, I describe her as a stager as she settled into running a successful franchise for eight years, before trying a childcare career while her daughter was small, and talks of taking on another franchise in the near future as it pays more. This pattern of easy movement and return to what worked earlier partly explains her categorisation as accepter. At the time of interview, however, she was working as a pre-school assistant in a one-to-one capacity, hence the job status code of 2. Looking across her indicator chain, all the codes are low ones. She had no higher-level capabilities that she could use cumulatively for advancement or to compensate for other weaknesses and thus her current ability to function is comparatively low-level (although her achievements on the course suggest the existence of yet undeveloped potential).

It would be possible to produce capability chains for all of the students to summarise their narratives for comparison purposes, and such a process suggests a later possibility of refining these codes to allow the development of fuller ordinal, even interval, scales. Here, my intention is merely to make visible how students' capability sets can vary over time, opening up different choices and leading to differing subsequent functionings. The capability chains also demonstrate that there is no simple correlation between personal qualities and outcomes, supporting my view that we should be wary of constraining people's choices, as we may be limiting their potential. Educational opportunities should be broader and courses available for all to try, enabling people to expand their capability sets.

Taking an overview

This chapter forms the theoretical core of the book. It defines the original integrated lives triangle in abstract and considers its relationship to other theoretical perspectives, finding support in the theories of greedy institutions and cognitive dissonance, little evidence of adaptive preference and partial links to social capital theory. Importantly, it presents an explanation of the capability approach with a particular focus upon the idea of the capability set, as, for mature women training to work in childcare, this 'set' is represented by the integrated lives triangle. Recasting the occupational typologies as a vertical array of career outcomes, and the attitudinal set as descriptors of agency, the chapter considers how themes recurring across the narratives could be valorised to serve as capability indicators and charted as capability chains to allow visual comparison between students. This adds to our understanding of the complexity of the process whereby capability turns into functioning and choices are realised. It also supports the claim that functioning cannot be predicted from a small selection of personal characteristics.

Taking a less theoretical stance, we should pause to consider why these connections matter. We have seen that the integrated lives theory makes sense of complex real world data but what does this theory offer back to society?

Firstly, it has taken the freely given personal accounts of mature students working in childcare and extracted significant common findings from their narratives without simplistic reduction or disrespect for their individual stories. This is significant, as so often theorising smoothes over difference and diversity, seeking an average or typical solution that holds good for no one at all. Importantly, the theory challenges common assumptions that women care for children because they can do nothing else. In demonstrating that women choose to balance different options in their lives, it provides an alternative to the commonly held deficit model of women's education that sees 'juggling' as a negative factor rather than a potential positive choice.

In showing that women from a diverse range of backgrounds share the desire to balance the needs of self, family, work and study, this theory challenges the stereotypical vision that women who work in childcare are a distinctive species: predominately undereducated, working class or mired in the profession. It also demonstrates that flexibility – in practices, working conditions, work-life boundaries – so often equated with a lack of professionalism, plays an important role in keeping local communities alive and thriving and in allowing the people who use facilities to play a part in organising and managing them. The theory demonstrates conclusively that part-time does not equate with second-best. Instead it presents a picture of real lives that originates in the community being studied rather than a remote theoretical perspective. This is a workable theorisation that takes into account the human values that matter in society and the advantages of this are further discussed in chapter 8. But first we need to look at the research data in more detail.

Chapters 1 to 4 have provided a policy context and a theoretical framework for this study but to substantiate the theory we need to leave the holistic analyses and examine and analyse the interview data. For simplicity I adopt a chronological structure, so chapter 5 examines the students' individual and collective experiences and expectations of education, focusing on events that preceded the Diploma course. Chapter 6 looks at practices and chapter 7 at the consequences of education. This longitudinal treatment assists the process of making sense of complex lives, drawing attention to the cumulative consequences of individual choices and confirming the importance of the freedom to choose.

5

Recalling experiences
and expectations

ollowing the theoretical analyses of chapters 3 and 4, this chapter begins to examine the evidence which allowed the typologies and the integrated lives triangle to be developed. To maintain chronological integrity, it starts with an examination of the ways the students referred back to their own childhoods, making connections across time to their decision to study again as adults. It was clear during the interviews that past experiences significantly affected expectations for adult education so this chapter explores both aspects, looking also at the students' family backgrounds.

Despite encouragement from their colleagues, students found returning to education quite a challenge. Many expressed apprehension about attending college. Ingrid, for example, claimed 'I don't do teenagers very well' and Irene, a graduate, was afraid of feeling 'out of place' in 'a predominantly young person college'. Those who had had poor experiences in the compulsory sector were particularly nervous. Irma found the prospect 'a bit daunting', Heidi found it 'nerve-wracking' and Heena admits: 'I was very frightened to go back to education because I'm not really very good at it'. Arianne's fears were more reflective: 'I was frightened I would be bored and not listen and then not be able to do the work'.

Like Arianne, many of them assumed that practices in adult education would be similar to those in the compulsory sector, and expected to be treated as a child:

> I felt I was going to sit there at a desk, be told off for talking, but no it was great. You could go to the loo when you had to ...'

Past personal experiences

Ten of the interviewees had thoroughly disliked school and fourteen had enjoyed it, leaving a further nine who viewed it neutrally. As might be expected, students who disliked school rarely stayed on to take A-levels although one, Greta, had after several false attempts achieved not only these but a degree as well. Childhood problems were very individualised but revealed the strength of links between family and education for young children. At a social level, poor educational practices included a failure to address power issues between students and between staff and students, and a lack of proper pastoral care. Organisational structures also created problems, centring on issues connected to streaming, even after comprehensive schooling was introduced in 1965. The concerns often demonstrated a rigid adherence to procedures and a lack of imagination on the part of the teachers, who failed to consider why students acted as they did.

Exceptional problems

Personal traumas affected their behaviour at school and eventually led some to fear the educational process. We saw in chapter 3 how Greta's experiences in a 'dame' school led to school failure and an inability to settle anywhere. Celia, isolated by her peers at secondary school, had a breakdown on entering sixth form, when she felt that 'the teachers were rejecting me as well'. Evelyn, reacting to a new baby in the family, had truanted from the age of 4 and 'left the moment I could'. In several cases, school staff could have intervened but chose instead not to question the behaviour. Fiona had struggled with a violent stepfather and 'skived' school but the teachers had merely laughed at her 'once a month class' when she attended to pick up work. Irma, challenged daily for rebellious behaviour, was never asked what was wrong so never disclosed that, living with a single and distressed parent, she had 'such an unhappy home life, it made school not important'. Faye told me at her interview about her difficult adolescence. Her mother died when she was 11 and she had to care for her younger brother and run the home: 'I took on the role of mum really'. She drifted through secondary school, possibly in a state of shock, and unaware of her adapted capability set. These students had all experienced exceptional difficulties but had found ways of coping with them before entering childcare work.

For a few, the problems were ongoing. Fiona experienced further trauma: not only did a key relative develop a terminal illness but she was also personally subjected to an armed attack on a garage forecourt. She dealt with these issues too, but they did precipitate a decision to enter paediatric nursing immediately: 'I don't want to die having never tried'. Irma used the Diploma course as a distraction while she tried to become pregnant again, but found the presence of small babies difficult. Three students saw education as a possible solution. Evelyn, treated for depression after leaving an abusive marriage, sought the confidence 'to do something' and colleagues in her group encouraged her to qualify. Holly, invalided out of the police force after being attacked in the cells, tackled agoraphobia by working alongside her children. This integration of family, work and education avoided one of her 'little blips' – having to return home alone after taking children to school. For Heena, the pre-school's expectations, 'you had to help out and be on the rota', encouraged her to seek help when she realised belatedly that she had become agoraphobic, her capability set reduced to home-based activities. Travelling to college alone was part of her self-imposed cure.

For Daisy, also, the Diploma offered resolution. Her plans to research theoretical physics were unachievable after she suffered a serious head injury but she remained passionate about education and determined to work in the field. She tried a teaching role and a teaching assistantship, but found pre-school work to be the most she could manage while her four children were growing up. Thus successfully completing the Diploma allowed her to work in educational settings. She is a strong believer in holistic education and sees childcare work as an extension of her mothering role: 'I love them like my own really'. Her life story exuberantly mixes family, work and educational values.

Failures of the system

No less than eight interviewees complained that they were bullied at school: Fiona and Avril for doing well, Arianne and Ilsa for their looks, Imogen and Arianne (again) as a result of moving house, Celia and Greta for being different from their peers and consequently friendless, Barbara, because one classmate disliked her. Teachers, too, did their share of bullying. Several of the students recall staff treating them in ways that would now lead to disciplinary proceedings. Holly (aged 40), a former police officer trained in child protection issues, recalls practices like shouting, enforced milk-drinking, 'whacked' knuckles, chalk and board rubber projectiles, and a 'horrible, horrible teacher who used to draw a big red line all the way through your book'; even a teacher who 'always used to be touching you'. Greta (aged 48) recalled the teacher in the 'dame' school she attended claiming that she had only recently stopped putting mustard on children's tongues. Celia (aged 49) traces her lack of confidence even now to 'a very strict primary headmaster' who humiliated errant students who could not remember their times tables. She went into 'a panic every single time we had tests', making punishment inevitable. Faye encountered similar problems.

Younger students had also found teachers unsupportive. Imogen (aged 21) claims: 'I was basically told I was stupid the whole way through'. She highlights the common complaint that middling students receive little attention: 'I wasn't *very* clever but I wasn't stupid either and I just got left out'. Imogen's problems, and Ilsa's too, cast some doubt on the efficacy of modern transfer routines where students entering secondary school are placed in forms with members of their primary class to ensure continuity. As Imogen explains, this policy is fine if students are happy in their primary schools. If not, it is disabling. In Ilsa's (aged 29) words, you are 'never actually removed from the situation'.

Some students linked their ambivalence towards education to former organisational practices. For two, the 11+ had been a source of strain as segregated schooling continued long past 1965. Ingrid (aged 49) claimed that failing selection made her feel inferior to her brother. Celia felt that being taunted throughout the last term of primary for failing the 11+ ruined her chances in secondary school. Others complained about restricted subject choice. Alex failed examinations and Frieda 'dropped out', both of them as a result of being forced to study too many academic subjects. Evelyn was denied cookery classes after moving house and changing schools, and Daisy still regrets that she could not do metalwork or woodwork – but she did get to study aeronautics. In the case of Heena it was her parents who wanted her to 'do a nice feminine subject' like home economics rather than the drama or pottery that she would have preferred.

Without doubt, such restrictive educational practices challenged the women's capability to achieve certain functionings in later life. Some students, however, claimed a personal role in limiting their options. Aileen described school as 'boring' and admits to doing little work. Avril and Barbara both mentioned a liking for boys that ruined their concentration and in the latter case, led to an early pregnancy (but also to a stable marriage and two more children, defying the generalisation that young mothers cannot cope). Celia developed an escape mechanism by daydreaming – which in effect prevented learning.

Collectively the small attritions – the bullying, the teacher humiliation, the moving house and parental separations, the difficulties in making and maintaining friendships, the sibling rivalry – played a significant role in reducing people's capability to act. Young children are very vulnerable to atmosphere and upset and they internalise challenging situations. Celia's recall of a comment made on moving from rural Wales to a London suburb at the age of 6 captures this process: 'Mummy they don't love me here like they used to in my old school'. Stressful situations lower children's self-esteem and sense of agency, vital factors in turning capability into functioning, but this is not to claim that every such change requires therapeutic intervention. Many children adjust and become stronger as a result of coping with change.

Embedded family values

A number of interviewees described their parents' influence on educational expectations: either by direct intervention or indirectly through embedded value systems. The instances are too few to permit generalisation but they do bear out prevalent class, gender and cultural norms, revealing an Asian and white middle-class concern that education is vital to future personal and economic success, a lower-class disinclination to invest in their children's future, and the favouring of male opportunity over female. The parental attempts to guide the student, whether these were valued or rejected, rarely led to successful outcomes. This possibly demonstrates the importance of human agency in the development of capabilities: parents can only facilitate their children's achievements, not create them. Alternatively, it could indicate that parental involvement is only memorable or confessable when the student retains some feelings of residual guilt. The parental comments, however, did alert me to consider students' background and early schooling when I was attempting to develop an understanding of how students come to have different capabilities and how this will affect their future functionings.

Class issues

Several parents interceded in the selection of secondary school. The background narratives of, respectively, horse-riding, strict convent schools, and catchments suggest middle-class aspirations. Despite the parents' efforts, none of these students achieved the A-level grades that the parents presumably sought. When Celia failed the 11+, her mother refused the secondary modern place and obtained a place for her at a technical high school where she was 'absolutely slaughtered' for her 'posh accent'. When Celia 'cracked up' after her O-levels, her mother had to intervene again, whisking her off to become a riding instructress.

Felicity's mother also chose an alternative school, favouring one some distance away from the local convent attended by Felicity's friends. Felicity settled quickly and seems to have worked hard up to the mock GCSEs, but failed to revise for the real exams, obtained lower-than-anticipated grades, and insisted on getting a job instead of staying on at school. She attributes this to her mother being too busy to notice: she was going through the break up of her 'second – or was it the third?' relationship.

Frieda's mother, who moved house to secure her daughter a place in an ex-grammar school, tried to contain her daughter's diminishing interest in academic study by suggesting a move to a sixth form college. Having achieved good GCSEs, Frieda elected to stay at school, lacking the confidence to 'break away'. She struggled with the workload and when the school refused to allow her to drop a subject, became 'quite disenchanted' and insisted on leaving at Easter with no further qualifications. Danni, also middle class, set the boundaries for herself, electing, 'probably against my better judgment', to leave school at 16 rather than be a financial burden. Age was the significant factor here: 'Dad was retired', his reduced income restricted Danni's capability set.

Conversely, for Bella it was her parents who set the firm boundaries that limited her educational opportunities. Here, too, a class element is evident. She describes her father as a factory worker, and her mother as without qualifications: 'I don't think they had got any'. Bella (an asserter) insisted on her need for sixth form study but could not progress beyond this point: 'it was never going to be on the cards for me to do more than A-levels certainly'. Evelyn's mother let her truant from the age of 4, and so frequently that the headteacher turned up in person to collect Evelyn. I suspect a class element here too, as the mother was clearly intimidated by the teacher and relieved that Evelyn had measles on this occasion: 'My mum did actually say, the relief on her that 'phew, she is actually ill' but very often I wasn't and I knew that once that bus went past I was home'.

The possible exception to this alignment of educational aspirations with class is Irma. Her transcript suggests a strongly working-class background but her mother insisted on attendance, punishing her when she 'bunked off once'. However, Irma's comment that 'I wasn't afraid of teachers or anything because my home life was a lot worse' makes it impossible to determine whether the maternal attitude was pro-school or merely punitive. Irma left school with six CSEs and no clear idea of what she could do next and moved haphazardly from one poorly paid job to another.

At a simple level these decisions demonstrate a middle-class aspiration for a good education and a working-class expectation of economic independence on reaching the minimum school-leaving age, suitably qualified or not. These working-class students had reduced educational capabilities: there was a tacit assumption that to have more than a basic education was a luxury.

Gender issues

Alex's story demonstrates how gender influenced educational decisions. She and her brother were treated very differently and as a result live contrasting lives. Alex went to the local comprehensive school, albeit one with a good reputation, but her brother was entered for a bursary at a local private school. She shows no resentment but I detect a slight irony when she says:

> My parents in their wisdom decided that he – it would most probably be more valuable for him to go rather than me and my sister.

Alex enjoyed school but 'really had her heart set on taking typing and sewing' for O-level and was dismayed when told by the headteacher that she had to take sciences instead. This seems particularly harsh, as these are traditional feminine subjects and Alex had been denied the opportunities reserved for the male in the family. As her parents were separating, familial support was limited, so she accepted the school decision but did not pass either chemistry or physics and left school at 16. She is now a single parent, bringing up two teenagers and working an early shift in a local newsagent's so that she can be free by 3pm when school finishes. She has a very positive outlook and a strong friendship network. Alex's story is about compassion and making choices for the good of her family but it is also, unusually, one of adaptive preference. Returning to the gender situation, we need to note that the brother achieved fourteen grade As at GCSE, studied further, and now has 'a house worth over half a million with five bathrooms in which he lives with his dog'. Alex prefers to have her children and claims: 'I don't see it is about money': a view that some of us might find difficult to share entirely.

Gender issues also figure in Ilsa's story. Her father insisted on her taking A-levels in order to enter the armed forces as an officer as, during his period of active service, female privates were bullied. Ilsa 'was brought up very strictly'. She talks about bad behaviour being 'drummed out of me' and would never have dared miss school or defy her father until she had no option. Having picked 'totally the wrong subjects', English literature and sociology, Ilsa came out with two Es at A-level. This student, who later became a drill instructor, one of very few women gaining entrance to this male domain, admits: 'I still like to be taught bang, bang, bang, bang, bang, no discussions, no stories, none of that, none of this going off at a tangent' so it is hard to imagine her succeeding with her chosen topics. Ironically, on applying to the armed forces she found she needed a better maths O-level, so freed by her new adult status she 'enlisted anyway' as a private and found that her father's fears were unfounded.

Cultural issues

The two Asian students interviewed, reflected cultural emphases in educational expectations. Heena is British-born, part of a first-generation immigrant family who expected her to conform to traditional norms for an arranged marriage but, eventually, accepted her right to choose her own husband – who is white British. She talks of being quite isolated at school: 'I couldn't really build on the social side of things because my parents were so strict'. She describes her parents' high expectations: 'the pressure at home was humungous to get a good education because of my culture'. Expectations, for girls at least, were inextricably linked to marriage prospects. Husbands were supposed to be better educated than wives so educating a daughter to higher levels raised the chances of securing a husband with better prospects. Here education and marriage are seen to fall within the same capability *vector* rather than being contradictory options. The traditional view of marriage or education for women is tinged with 21st century realism, even a recognition that marriage may not work out – tellingly, Heena also mentions that independence is important.

Heena describes a strict childhood, short on luxuries and toys as her parents were saving towards their three daughters' education. Her father expected her to work hard and it is clear that although at one level she knew his comments like 'there's a rope in the loft, should your results be bad' and 'you are just going to spend the rest of your life packing boxes in the supermarket' were rhetorical rather than real threats; at another level she understood their serious import: 'I just thought, no, I've got to do it, I've got to do it, I've got to do it'. Declaring herself 'politically incorrect', she describes the value system of her local community, favouring medicine, then pharmacy, then optometry as careers. Exam failure, 'my one little E', limited her HE options to a computing diploma at a university where it was intended she would find a partner: 'the man, the husband that they wanted me to try to get married to went there'. The plan backfired, Heena 'met my husband instead'. Her parents disowned her and then repented (her mother after a day, her father after six to eight months), but she admits to a long period of post-natal agoraphobia, suggesting that the struggle for independence was more stressful than her cheery retelling implies. She also emphasises the importance of choice, still regretting that she was not allowed to develop capabilities in the arts or practical subjects.

Hansa, in contrast, is a temporary UK resident, educated to degree-level in her own country. Hansa explains how, at home, parents insist on young children learning to read and write early, that competition for secondary and higher education is very stiff and that families will sell up and 'sacrifice everything', to live in crowded conditions in cities where there are good schools and colleges. 'I think fifty per cent of people, they do not have a life, they are always behind the children.' From a Western cultural perspective this appears to be *distorting* rather than integrating lives: a view that the student herself seems to share, as she has experienced life in Britain.

Taken together, these scenarios demonstrate a range of interlinkages. They show how the ability to achieve in education is affected by serious personal or family traumas, by chronic social and cultural divisions embedded in society, but also by restrictive practices and lack of support within schools. Family intervention cannot make children learn but can very easily prevent them from doing so. The narratives demonstrate that negative experiences have a long lasting effect: the students who said they were happy at school did not offer details or examples, whereas those who had unhappy experiences were keen to retell them at length. It is possible the students felt the need to tell what Geoffrey Baruch (1981, citing Stimson and Webb, 1975) terms 'atrocity stories' (cc) to convey their satisfaction with the Diploma course and their awareness of how much education has changed, but equally possible that they needed a cathartic opportunity. It was noticeable that the students who still had existing issues to contend with told their stories slowly, sometimes needing help in recognising what the problem was. This was an area where I had to take care not to lead the discussion, only to ask for clarification.

Compulsory education leaves lasting impressions on children that colour their views of adult education and influence their inclination to undertake further study later.

Maternal identity

For most of the interviewees the role of mother formed part of their core identity. It was apparent throughout the research that the needs of family were foregrounded whenever a decision had to be made. However, we see in the next chapter that although many families actually offered a range of practical assistance to the students, the students did not demand this. Students constructed a central support role for themselves within the family and there is plentiful evidence that they did not like their study commitments disrupting this or isolating them from their children. Felicity talks of feeling guilty and 'missing out on spending time with them'. Daisy describes her 'worst Sunday' when she was 'locked up in the bedroom doing an assignment' and '*all* my family were downstairs'. Danni gave up her subsequent degree course, ostensibly because the 'children weren't happy' but also because studying made life 'too stressful', suggesting that there is more than altruism at play here. It could well be an example of Festinger's (1957) cognitive dissonance in operation, the process whereby psychological conflict is avoided by changing one attitude to fit another.

Generally, the students were very anxious not to disrupt the smooth running of the household. Frieda claimed to 'scuttle around' because studying 'wasn't to affect anything else'. Faye described how 'family life was first for me really' and was keen not to compromise it. Celia described how 'I *did* feel obliged to do everything else around the house and do the work at some ridiculous time of night'. Even for those who demonstrated an ability to prioritise and plan ahead the discourse centred on cheating on the housework: 'I didn't vacuum every day' and 'sometimes the washing was left out for two days on end' (Beryl). We saw (in chapter 1) that most of the students (more than 80%) were married and it seems that they also subscribed, at least partially, to the Victorian view of the patriarchal family. It is claimed that, despite neo-conservative attempts to resurrect core family values, by the mid-1990s the traditional roles of male breadwinner and non-working economically dependent wife 'no longer typified' Britain (Arnot, David and Weiner, 1999:91). My findings suggest that the women working in childcare were only one step away from that pattern. Most earned wages that were insignificant compared to the salary of the breadwinner.

Vocational reasons for working in childcare
Income
In most contemporary workplaces, employees work to formal job descriptions that clearly set out contractual obligations. These often include a general clause covering 'any reasonable additional duties' and senior staff are usually expected to carry out such tasks flexibly as they arise. The interesting anomaly with childcare workers in the voluntary sector, as we see later, is that many appear to honour the flexible working practices and commitment of professional workers but are prepared to do so on rates of pay, which are barely above the minimum wage. As Bethany said, it is 'a full-time job with part-time pay'. However, none of the students implied that the money they earned represented an element of independence or luxury. Even Amy, who said she 'didn't need to work for the money', failed to make this connection. Nor was autonomy stated as a reason, although Emily pointed out that she was paid less than a teaching assistant despite having 'lots of responsibility'. This raises interesting questions about motivation, for the students on the Diploma course came from a broad range of social and educational backgrounds and many could have made different choices.

There is evidence that money does matter – but not in the short term. Students move into parallel positions that pay better, when the time is right. Beryl managed to achieve this even before the end of the course, asking for a reference even while handing in her final assignment, as she 'needed something that actually showed that I was getting some reward for what I was doing'. Felicity took a new job because she wanted 'some money to spare'. Gina, a graduate who could earn much more, sees the work as 'perfect for what I want at the moment', but not necessarily in the longer term: 'if it was well paid ... I probably wouldn't think of moving. I'm quite happy'. Only Irma, who is leaving the profession, directly sets salary against job role and indignantly asks: 'I do sometimes think, if I'm honest, what am I doing, £6 an hour, wiping someone's bum and snotty noses, honestly, while my stomach's heaving?'

If salary is not the key reason for working in childcare, what are the motives?

Altruism

Some students justified low remuneration by recasting their role as community support. Perhaps this is a facet of the gradual transition from volunteer to worker. Heena accepted poor pay 'because it's a charity'. Frances 'wanted to help the community and the mothers that perhaps couldn't do that'. Danni, too, considered other families' needs: 'You've got some parents who, if we increase the fees, just couldn't send their children anywhere'.

These comments raise the question of whether some women choose childcare as a career because it is a good cause. By willingly working for very little, they possibly engender a feeling of self-worth. Certainly Danni was involved in voluntary work from an early age following her mother's dictum that 'if you want to see something happen, you get involved, and that is still very much what I believe'. Danni is heavily involved in the school parent teacher association and the church, as well as the pre-school, but all in a neighbouring village. When I question whether this geographical displacement allows her to maintain an element of distance she hesitates but is honest enough to accept that this could be the case: 'Probably ... yes that is probably true'. Danni seeks a sense of belonging, but not too much of it.

In her interview Evelyn not only expressed personal altruism but also revealed how this caused conflict between herself and a new manager who 'wanted paying for every single thing she did'. Evelyn would appear to work for personal esteem rather than a salary. She actually says: 'For me, my reward isn't the pay', and going into the local school as a teaching assistant (TA) continues this pattern of quasi-working quasi-volunteering.

I went into work on Sunday for two hours ... and I won't get paid for it. But I don't expect to get paid for it because I know that a job needed doing and ... that's a big satisfaction ... nobody knows I went in apart from the teachers that I worked with ... but I know that I went in and I've done my best.

On reflection, the passage above raises the possibility that Evelyn may be seeking recognition by, even parity with, colleagues in addition to a sense of self-worth. Later in the interview she describes offering to carry out an observation on a child with special needs and concludes: 'And it is quite nice when they think, oh yes, she's not as daft as she looks'.

Wanting to work with children

Although 80 per cent of participants ticked 'wanting to work with children' as an option on the background questionnaire (see chapter 1), few mentioned this as their main motivating factor. In the interviews the emphasis was on 'what I can do next', implying, in capability terms, an acceptance of what is possible. Exceptionally, Frieda admits: 'there is something about that age group that I still find exciting even though my children have moved on from it'. Fiona was focused on children's needs rather than just her own career and, as we saw in chapter 3, pursued a career in neonatal nursing. Imogen, a young adult just post-A-level, showed a real commitment to young children: 'I like working with children, I like figuring them out'. She believes that this is an essential requirement for a career in childcare: 'you have either got the passion and the people who haven't got it complain about money, complain about doing things, and cleaning, and doing their job'. Unfortunately, her work setting, a day nursery, was poorly managed and unsupportive and she decided to register for a psychology degree instead of continuing to work in childcare. Because she already had A-levels, she had the capability to chose a different functioning and, with no children of her own, had no need to integrate her life closely. Family was important to Imogen but had a different role: her parents were prepared to support her through university.

Truly liking children was seldom enough to sustain a childcare career. Heidi, for example, expressed a sincere 'attachment' to children, and wanted to 'be able to help every child'. She struggled to qualify, only completing the Diploma on her third attempt, and was no longer working in the group when interviewed. There had clearly been problems with other staff and the committee and possibly with an Ofsted inspection too. Heidi's plans are inconsistent, tingeing idealism with realistic doubts and it seems likely that it is this combination of emotions that made running a group so difficult for her. She talks of setting up a supermarket crêche, of working at the local hospital, of buying the pre-school outright if she won the lottery, and her claim that she would be an excellent reception teacher is very effusive. But moments later she admits: 'I'm a bit scared and don't know what way to go'. Frances, the agoniser described in chapter 3, really cared about children but left childcare because it 'messed her head'. Diane and Celia, who just wanted to 'play' with children, disliked management responsibilities and moved out of childcare. Imogen (mentioned above) moved on because she wanted a better environment for children: 'because I *care*, it is always going to *bother* me'.

Others who talked about play but continued to work in childcare articulated the link between play and education, thereby demonstrating a more realistic awareness of expectations. Ingrid was fascinated to find young children to be 'like little sponges', who 'soak up knowledge so much' and recognised that you need to be educated to 'look after other people's children'. Aileen found observation methods 'fun' because 'you actually get to see how a child's mind works'. Emily worried that 'we're not getting down with the children and *learning* through play'. Cindy, too, stressed the importance of play: 'even though they are playing they are still learning'. These students recognised that children's capability formation is optimised when the environment is relaxed and age-appropriate.

Professionally, many students understood the importance of play for children but challenged the misconception that they themselves were playing with children rather than working. Ilsa was very indignant that armed forces personnel 'just think a load of women rock up and look after kids in a big room for hours' and Deirdre gets very annoyed 'when my husband says you only just play with children'.

Not planning a career

One possible explanation for the low priority given to both income and children as motivating factors was the casual way that students entered the profession: volunteering led to jobs. Diane's comment is fairly representative of those who drift into work like this and is echoed by Amy, Aileen, Avril, Alex and Daisy:

> I volunteered to be secretary ... and then I was treasurer for two years ... and then the pre-school was looking for extra help and asked me if I would like to come back and help ... I found myself on the books as an employee before I knew it.

Heena describes the process vividly when she talks of 'capturing the mum market'.

For housewives it's like a step into using the brain again, something they know because they've got their own children.

Very few of those who made the transition from parent to long-term practitioner intended to do this. Amy had 'no career plans', Emily didn't mean to 'get so heavy into childcare' and nor did Avril and Arianne. Faye, too, claims: 'If you had said to me five years before that I would be working with children ... I would have said Never'. Ironically, Alex who 'did at the time' want a career, was one of the people who quickly returned to a retail job, needing more money as a single parent. Daisy, however, remarked how she saw Diploma students 'become more professional' and by implication desired a similar personal transformation. She wanted to develop a new functioning.

Exceptionally, a number of students commented on teaching as a possible progression route from pre-school work. Graduates possessed the capability to achieve this function relatively easily but for some (Gina, Hansa, and Irene) it was only a vague future possibility, and others (Daisy and Greta) had considered it and decided it was not for them. Accepters Bethany and Felicity, both non-graduates, also contemplated teaching as a possible long-term goal, but accumulater Avril chose a more achievable functioning instead, by moving into the post-compulsory sector, where she did not need a degree to teach. Teaching is a considered aim for other accumulaters.

Barbara has teaching in mind as a long-term goal, is completing a foundation degree and 'doing it all backwards'. She became pregnant at 16, achieved a handful of CSEs, married and went on to have two more children; so the childcare Diploma was her first serious qualification. She is now actively compensating for her truncated schooling and repairing her self-esteem. Another accumulater, Holly, is working her way through the teaching assistant qualifications but is not yet sure whether teaching will be her ultimate goal, leaving that decision until the children are 'a tadge' older. This is another instance of the centrality of children to decision-making.

Apart from Holly, most of the students working as TAs eschew teaching. Beryl (a graduate) has decided not to develop this capability: 'not after seeing all the heartache and hair-tearing that seems to go on'. Evelyn admits to having the 'education bug' but 'would not want to be a teacher for love nor money these days'. Aileen focuses on the workload: 'they've got reports to write, they've got IEPs [Individual Education Plans], they've got work to mark and work to put together and planning and *no*, that's not me'. Arianne does not want to teach but clearly measures her own achievements against those of teachers and is uncomfortable if parents address her as such 'in front of any teachers that come'. 'I don't want them to think that we think that highly of ourselves.' Their unprompted talk about rejecting teaching implies an earlier consideration of this career: the students are aware of the choices forming their capability set.

Drifting into employment

The routes through which the students achieved employment in childcare often demonstrate the link between family and work as well as reinforcing the casual nature of the process. Sometimes the progression is fortuitous, more often a result of signalling interest. For Bethany, her child's behaviour was the trigger for involvement. The child would 'kick up or make a stink' and Bethany would hang around to settle her, and this led gradually to helping 'if they were short-staffed' and then to 'more permanent' work. Aileen 'sort of tagged along' with her daughter. Barbara moved from cleaner to committee member to worker when her son went to school and 'a job vacancy came up'. Celia 'started being a mother helper' and 'shifted over into a job when an opportunity came up'. As her daughter was 'just rising 3' it was convenient to work 'next door in the other classroom'. Both Barbara and Celia reveal the interdependence of family and work decisions.

Often the parent wanted social contact. Felicity 'really liked being part of a group', and wanted to 'integrate into the village'. Bella sought stimulation. She talked of not 'being able to relax' and described how, by dint of arriving early, she managed to progress from helper, to stand in, to paid helper. Ilsa made a purely instrumental decision to go into childcare to suit her family situation – young children and a husband still in the armed forces. Having considered nursing, hairdressing and childcare, she favoured the latter 'because we had a pre-school on camp where I knew I could go and do voluntary work'. Her husband funded the course so that she could start immediately, anticipating a future need to link family and work.

Some interviewees reacted promptly to opportunity. Evelyn says 'they offered me the job and I grabbed it'; Gina that 'after I'd volunteered for a while a one-to-one support post came up and I automatically took that'. Irma, in contrast, saw it as an alternative to being bored at home and responded to a friend's suggestion: 'Can't see why not'.

Several people were persuaded to try the job almost against their will, demon-strating that sometimes the element of choice is compromised when turning capability into functioning. Bethany and Danni were both coaxed into service, as their groups could not recruit leaders. Interestingly both students are still running these same, very successful, groups and work in close partnership with their local primary schools: their potential or capability to *be* and *do* was recognised by others and has been realised or functionalised through others. This is partly true, too, for Ingrid who was invited to join the pre-school by a friend and underwent a rapid conversion: 'it was just so different from how I expected it to be that I really, really enjoyed it'.

In contrast, Irene, a graduate who started the course as a volunteer and was immediately approached about a job as a playleader in a group that needed major restructuring, had 'a really tough year'. She has handed in her notice and 'planned that I might have a few months off' despite already being approached by two new employers. Again this decision was presented in terms of neglecting her family commitments: 'I thought the age my children are and how much time it is taking up and it didn't seem right for me to be carrying on'. But my persistent probing finally elicited other reasons: problems with the committee, acrimonious arguments about space and ratios for the following year, annoyance that as a trained worker she finds it 'hard not being listened to' and how this culminated in 'a bit of an email battle over Christmas'. That the group had approached her in the first place was an exacerbating factor. By withdrawing, she has exercised choice and her functioning has reverted to a capability. Financially, Irene did not need to work and the sacrifice involved in being less available for her own children was only acceptable when she was enjoying her work.

The lack of career planning combined with the drift into childcare work characterises a group of students who are realistically, sometimes instinctively, aware of the nature of their capability sets and who decide to turn possibilities into functionings. Their motivation for entering childcare seems to stem from recognition that this kind of work is amenable and possible: it is not a challenge to the role of motherhood. Many focus quite openly on the convenient nature of the work.

Convenience

Heena finds pre-school work 'handy'. Irma claims 'it fits in great with my daughter's school'. Gina finds the job 'perfect for what I want at the moment' and Bethany knew that she 'wanted to do something that would enable me to spend time with the girls'. Avril 'was interested' in childcare but acknowledges that 'it fits around your own children'. Arianne is now a manager and claims that 'the family comes first' for all her staff .

All of these girls, do this job because it goes well with the children.

People voice the importance of the short working day in a number of ways. Celia will '*not* go into work ... before my children have gone to school'. Cindy talks of being able to 'branch out' when her daughter went to school. Deirdre went looking for 'a job term time only', Daisy 'to fit in with the children really'. Frieda acknowledges the suitable hours, the school holidays and geographical proximity but describes these as a 'real bonus' rather than key factors. Felicity reveals that for her the process was also dual-motivated:

> I love working with the children and, yes, it started off with being very, very convenient in terms of fitting in with my family and in terms of its location ...

A few are clear that they want to avoid others caring for their children. Faye, Arianne, Bella and also Heena's husband overtly state this – but not as a criticism of daycare facilities

Dianne, Holly and Amy are among those who are able to put family above economic considerations. Others want to but cannot. Daisy, for example, observes: 'unfortunately when you are poor you realise that money does matter'. One student views financial considerations slightly differently. Cindy sees the low pay as a sign that people are 'dedicated to working with children' because 'there are more jobs, better paid, less qualification, that you could do'. She mentions stacking shelves in a supermarket as a better-paid option. Casual retail work is a viable alternative to childcare and several students had undertaken such work. Before going into childcare Fiona had worked in a supermarket. Hansa worked evenings to finance the course and her husband's continuing studies. Ingrid had had shop jobs while her first two children were young. Cara took up supermarket work immediately on completing the Diploma as it paid better and she needed to earn more.

Holly believes that convenience is a key factor but also that once established in childcare, people become apathetic towards moving on.

> For most women I would suggest that they are in childcare positions because it works for them while their children are young and then they get stuck in this rut and so they carry on.

My data show this is true of some of the accepters, also some agonisers, but not of most step-uppers and accumulaters: these students exercise human agency to turn capabilities into functionings.

Conversely, some students – Aileen, Deirdre, Faye – who wanted or needed to work, saw childcare as a bridge between their private and public lives. Aileen is explicit about her family priorities: 'It was more to fit in with family commitments ... That came first rather than the working conditions and salaries'.

Likewise, Evelyn clearly articulates her aim to balance conflicting needs and her recognition that her options are limited, her capability set shaped by compromise.

> I want the best of both worlds. I want to be able to work and also I want to be at home with my children when they are at home. And childcare, teaching, working within that environment allows me to do that and it's rewarding ...

Educational perspectives

So far, we have looked at students' educational narratives in relation to personal, familial and vocational expectations. Equally important are their philosophical views about education. What did students think education was for?

When asked directly about the purposes of education, students offered a range of answers which demonstrated an awareness of theoretical and practical, vocational and liberal polarities. Key values stated theoretically included the instrumental – vocational and functional issues (skills) – and a range of more liberal values, like personal aims for greater confidence and enjoyment of education for its own sake, expressed at times as 'fun'. Felicity, who held a liberal view of education, thought it was 'different for children and for adults', as children need to be taught a broad range of subjects as a preparation for adulthood. Sen too, according to Saito (2003:26), believes that 'restricting the temporary freedom of a child may well expand the freedom that the child will have in future'.

Vocational aims

As all the students had enrolled on the Diploma, itself a vocational training course, one might have expected vocational values to predominate. This was not the case: only two students, Deirdre and Heena, gave answers that were purely work-related. A further five students prioritised vocational issues but then introduced other matters. Bethany felt that 'if you didn't learn anything about anything you'd be a very dull person', Bella talked about 'personal goals', and Irene talked about the importance of 'learning something new'. She does not believe 'education should ever stop' but admits to currently needing a vocational motive in order to find the time to study:

> I think I work better if it's for a career purpose ... When I've got loads of time (laughs) doing something that's more of an interest is a more viable interest. Perhaps when the children are a lot older?

Faye merged theory and practice, seeking the ability to 'go out there and do something and to have that background behind it', and Ingrid recognises that education increases confidence and this helps you to 'get a better job'. Evelyn and Gina sought confidence in both the workplace and in interpersonal relationships, demonstrating mixed motives.

Functional skills and relevance

Four students focused on functional aspects of education. Avril, an adult education lecturer and Barbara, a foundation degree student may have been reiterating government policy. For Irma, however, skills acquisition was a personal need as she lacked basic IT skills and was encountering academic jargon for the first time: 'bibliography and all that sort of thing – I'd never heard of that before in my life'.

Aileen was less needy but this was largely because she had already made good a personal educational deficit. Working class, she left school at 16, 'had a couple of office jobs that I really hated', became pregnant and went back to college at 18 to do GCE maths to compensate for a low grade CSE. Concerned about continuing poor functional skills in society, she went to work as a primary school TA responsible for literacy and numeracy support when her pre-school folded. From a historical standpoint, her 'mission' resonates with the ideals of the radical educators. She is concerned that 'there are a few people around still that can't read and write and do basic sums' and insists that this should be addressed.

Aileen also believes that education should be relevant to life. She complains about the theoretical component of the Diploma syllabus: 'when do I ever use the theorists in the classroom?' only partly in jest. However, her awareness that education should be appropriate for purpose slightly broadens this perspective. She recognises that 'some people do educational courses just for the fun of it' but that others 'need a qualification'. Fiona raises a similar point about options, distinguishing between vocational and recreational needs in terms of people finding 'their own level'. Heidi, too, sees relevance to everyday life as intrinsically important and links this to children's ages. She favours a holistic play-based curriculum for little children:

> Just exploring is most important to children, being able to get outside and lift up boulders and rocks and that and see what's underneath them and explore why there're clouds moving in the sky.

Heidi stresses the importance for older children to be able to do 'something that they are actually interested in rather than something that they have to do'; but she assumes that this will be work-related. She is very negative about her children's experiences in the secondary sector and talks about peer pressure and how school tends to highlight the difference between the affluent and the rest – families like her own with reduced capabilities – leading to lower levels of functioning.

> As they get older, children are open to such different worlds ... you've got the children that go round bragging that they've done it all and been there, and you've got the children that wish they had done it all and been there.

Such a view should be considered alongside other claims that a key purpose of education is to boost confidence. When Walker (2006b:168) states that 'education is in itself a basic capability which affects the development and expansion of other capabilities' she is implying a positive role, not the reverse. Irene makes a similar point in lay terms when she says: 'you've got more opportunities if you, if you have qualifications'.

Liberal views

The majority of students took a broadly liberal view of education, often including vocational issues but in a secondary role or in relation to individual values and personal growth. Gina, who has experienced both types of education, believes that the vocational and liberal 'tie in anyway', Greta thinks it would be a 'lovely world where you can marry the two' and Danni firmly believes that without 'the underpinning [knowledge] sometimes the vocational doesn't have much value'. Some students were ambivalent about the relative worth of vocational and liberal education, possibly picking up messages from the media and central government. For example, Frieda who sees education as primarily liberal: 'to discover more about things and about yourself', admits that if she were studying 'for the sake of it' she would need a clear goal, to see a 'means to an end'. She goes on to say that this could be a career goal 'but it could be *just* personal development'. The word 'just' is ambiguous, as it could imply a separation of the vocational and personal or that the latter is inferior. In context, I think it spans the two meanings.

Many of the women although not all were returning to work after having children and so were acutely conscious of issues of confidence and self-esteem. Given the child-centred nature of the Diploma course, the focus on individualism and growth was perhaps inevitable. References to 'moving on', 'growing' and 'progression' were common; possibly connected to the long supremacy of Piaget's stages of development within childcare. Certainly several students (Alex, Beryl, Fiona) made colloquial reference to education's cognitive role: it 'expands the brain'. For Arianne progression carries notions of lifelong learning: 'you need ongoing teaching and learning and training in it to actually keep up with the world'. Her description also has a compensatory flavour, suggesting perhaps that second chances may only lead to second best:

> I'm sure if I was taught better at school or sent to a better school or was listened to at home ... I would probably have wanted to go into teaching ...

Poignantly, Celia not only talks about 'moving on in one's life and growing' but also – and note the element of uncertainty – says that 'you can move on and become a new person, a different person, hopefully?' When interviewed, Celia's life was at a crossroads. She had just decided to give up her job in a pre-school with an irascible manager 'after ten years treading on glass' because her marriage was 'falling apart' and she could not 'handle the two at once'. Her plans were to take time out and experiment with writing and illustrating children's books rather than any new educational initiative. Another student, Holly, also describes education in terms of life-style change, turning the theoretical question into an individualised one, a search for 'a different me as well'.

Some of the adults holding liberal views of education declared it enjoyable. Hansa found pleasure in reading and exploring things and graduated in biology because she really liked the subject. However, her decision to enrol on the childcare Diploma was differently motivated. An Asian student, living in England on a limited income while her husband completed his PhD, she needed a job. Thinking laterally, she decided that a childcare course would simultaneously improve her language skills, employability and self-assurance, thereby developing her capability to work in England. For her the key lay in the reading of 'simple books' to children.

Four students take a holistic view of education. Celia, who actually uses the word, mentions developing the 'whole person', Danni speaks of 'making links across different areas'. Heidi talked passionately about educational principles but, referring to the compulsory sector, saw this as largely negative. Daisy, the student who 'loves learning', has a holistic view of life as well as learning, and would like education not to be so 'single-minded'. She embraces 'deep' learning processes and says of the Diploma: 'some things you learn and you are not the same afterwards'. In general, the students' comments are very insightful, covering a far broader range of ideas than I could possibly include in this text. Insights like 'it's a civilising influence' (Amy), that it is to 'keep up with the world' (Arianne), or 'to help them understand themselves' (Cindy), deserve more attention than can be given here.

Overall, many students reveal themselves to be knowledgeable about educational theory and purposes but challenged emotionally, struggling to overcome negative familial and educational experiences and acquiring confidence through following the example of other parents who drifted into childcare ahead of them. The majority like the notion of studying for pleasure, the liberal ideal of education for its own sake, but recognise that for them this would be a luxury since they have such busy lives. Thus they demonstrate both realism and flexibility with regard to education, recognising that an element of compromise is essential if they are to balance the differing demands upon their time. Their commitment to children and family is visible in their readiness to fit their study time around obligatory household chores without being resentful. They foreground convenience, a sense of self-worth and fruitful occupation over receiving a satisfactory rate of pay, showing that they are motivated by human values rather than economic considerations *per se.*

Altogether, we are seeing complex patterns of interaction and dependence, with maternal and family roles, work in childcare, and educational qualification coming together supportively, to allow students to integrate their lives. In the next chapter we look at practices – in the home, the workplace and the classroom – and examine how the students' expectations and their semi-voluntary status affected their experience of adult education.

6

Examining educational practices

In chapter 5 we saw that their prior experiences left many students with negative expectations of education. This chapter starts by examining how easily students settled into college and the processes involved in *becoming* a student. It explores their coping strategies and levels of support within the family and the pre-school, but also looks at practices within the workplace and the classroom, ascertaining the students' views on the issues that are important to them. They generally focus on the period of study but at times stretch the time frame to include the period between study and interview.

In capability terms, this is a significant chapter. It discusses practices within education and in the personal, domestic and vocational spheres, focusing on the *beings* and *doings* of students' lives within college, in the home and in the workplace. In exploring how the students manage conflicting demands, this chapter begins the process of recognising constraints and possibilities, providing evidence that the students are freely choosing their functionings from an appropriate capability set.

Personal coping strategies
Becoming a student
Firstly we must look at the students' affiliation to college. Beryl's comment that 'we didn't think of ourselves as college students, more as people that just came in and did our bit and went away again' was echoed by others, so appeared to have broader validity. Belonging operated at the level of classroom rather than institution. For many of the students the adult nature of their class was vitally important. Ingrid, for example, who said (chapter 5): 'I don't do teenagers very well' was 'quite happy to be working with girls that were relatively round my age range, mature'. So too were Cindy, Felicity and

graduate Irene. All had enjoyed school, as had Frances who found college attendance 'a real treat' and Bella who found it 'quite energising'.

For students with less happy memories of school, the transition to student was less easy. Heena, who struggled with agoraphobia, coped by staying in the classroom: 'you are pretty much within your group anyway so you are not seeing a lot of the college'. Irma depended upon peer support: 'once I got into the room with the women, I felt fine'. The least positive comment came from Ilsa, the ex-forces drill instructor who had 'always worked with men'. She described *working* with women as 'horrendous' but felt that '*studying* with women' was slightly better 'because you are not there to socialise or really talk'. Aileen, too, distinguishes between working with and studying with women, and also preferred the latter option.

> In an office you are all doing your different jobs ... but on a course ... you are all doing the same things and we had a good laugh and got on really well with each other.

This element of shared experience is mentioned repeatedly. Avril and Arianne both talk of everyone being 'in the same boat' and even Heidi who, unlike the others, found the group a threat, realised that you 'always settle after a while'.

Celia and Danni saw college as an escape from the stresses of the workplace: respectively claiming 'a day out' and 'a day when I could *not* worry about what was going on at work as well'. Once she overcame her initial apprehension, Arianne found 'the actual college bit ... quite good fun'. This contrasts with her school days, when she was bullied and when 'the main object of the day was getting through it unscathed'. She acknowledged that 'the thought of going back to college was harder than the actual work at college', verbalising the long-term consequences of poor compulsory schooling identified in the previous chapter.

Forming groups

We saw that it mattered to students to be amongst other adults, and other aspects of group support were also important on a course like the Diploma. Avril points out: 'they like coming to the group; they don't like the course ending ...'. Bella mentions the importance of 'the bond you get as it goes on' and several interviewees mention the importance of support from fellow students. Cindy generalises this, noting that in a small group in college, 'you can help each other out'. This is in contrast to the experience of being in a larger group.

Despite my considerable efforts to move and mix students, the cohorts divided themselves into comfortable sub-groups, often according to ability or background. Heidi remarked on the way people found their niche by forming 'little groups', claiming that she herself had settled with the 'less educated' group. Another member of the same cohort, Holly, who described the class as 'lively and friendly', also noticed the factions – a group she 'sat alongside', students she did not 'always see eye-to-eye with' and others who 'all went and smoked together'. Despite repeated movement for groupwork, students in cohort 'I' also maintained their preferred positions. Ilsa talks of the classroom being 'quite separated' and openly labels sub-groups according to their ethnicity, class, age and self-esteem, placing herself among 'your kind of normal people at the back'. However, most students enjoyed the diversity within the group – as Emily specifically mentions:

> There was a lot of mixed abilities, high achievers there who found it very easy ... they had been to University whatever, and there were others who maybe dropped out of school so it was quite interesting and also if anybody did ... we were quite ... helping each other. I think it was a friendly course, and there were quite a lot of us, but I thought it was quite friendly.

Finding a friend

Deirdre saw herself as brave because she turned up alone. She draws attention to a significant feature of the course, the practice of either coming with a friend or making a friend or informal 'study buddy'. Several students formed supportive pairs. Arianne came on the course with Alice, travelled to college with her and studied with her in the evening: 'we would do it between us and it was fine'. Greta also derived benefit from attending with a colleague. She lived some distance from college and had no transport apart from a bike. Her colleague drives but 'doesn't like new experiences and was very glad to have someone with her'. As Greta jokingly put it: 'our phobias matched!' Deirdre, who found studying very hard, 'wouldn't have done it without the people at the course to help me' and talks about going round to one student's house for assistance. Pairing can also create stress, however. Irma only enrolled on the course because her graduate friend was doing it, but 'didn't want to look thick in front of her'. Consequently, when Irma needs help it is to her partner and to another, different, friend that she turns.

Looking horizontally across the cohort of 150 students I could identify nine such study pairs. Looking vertically, only three interviewees referred to earlier students specifically but I know that some pre-schools sent me a succession of students, indicating that recruitment is probably informed by hearsay within the early years settings. In effect, students who find pathways that lie within their capability sets identify the successful routes to others. Every student had to find her own way of working however, carving study time within busy lives.

Patterns of studying

As a perennial late night student myself, I was at first surprised that only two students mentioned 'burning the midnight oil' and only seven studied late – and then only when assignments were due in. Perhaps mature students prefer to study during the day, as they are already accustomed to regular working hours. Certainly Irene, the 'holiday' worker, avoided reading late at night once she had small children but said she had done this as an undergraduate.

> I could do that when I was at university but with young children getting up early in the morning I just can't function properly if I do that.

Heidi, Ingrid, Irma, Alex, Faye and Celia, who admits to crying in the night over assignments, studied late at night. They all did so only to avoid disrupting the family and not from choice. As Faye remarked, it was not something to be repeated. Arianne worked on her day off and in the evening but had a relaxed approach to learning and happily recalled 'sitting and reading it in bed at night when the children had gone to bed'. Other students deliberately excluded late night study, Diane was a 'before 9 o'clock' student and Frieda claimed that 'my brain and my body shut down by about 8.30' and described getting up at about 6 or 7am on a Sunday morning 'because it didn't affect anyone or affect a day out at all', adding that she 'would be lying in bed worrying about it anyway'.

Students frequently mentioned cramming study into every possible moment. Alex, Barbara, Felicity and Gina described doing so and Ingrid deliberately avoided regular routines, preferring to 'dash up and go and do an hour' when she had 'got it in your head, rather than doing stipulated times'. Aileen talked of 'always' having the assignments 'out on the living room floor' and doing work 'when I could'. Beryl, a graduate like Gina, also had the discipline to use odd times effectively: 'times when you might have just sat down and have a cup of tea, you just had to get on'. Bella prioritised study over housework, using 'windows of opportunity' to work systematically but still needing a 'final sort of splurge' at the end to pull an assignment together. She says she 'just became a hermit really' as, living in a small isolated community, she had to discourage other mums from dropping in.

You sort of have to put people off and say 'I've got assignments to do. I really need to *not* see you this week or next week'.

Many of the students were still working part-time and could utilise their unpaid time during the week to study: Arianne, Barbara, Bella and Felicity talked of having a day off; Frieda, Diane and Evelyn said they had an afternoon off that they could use; Aileen had a couple of afternoons; Bethany studied while her daughter had an afternoon nap. Personality and circumstances rather than prior experience appeared to dictate study patterns. Of the graduates, Amy seemed to find study time effortlessly, perhaps because 'the kids were all at school full time'. Beryl was very disciplined. Gina, however, left everything to the last minute: 'I need the adrenalin to kick in'. So did Daisy, who hated missing out on family life: 'I didn't find enough time to do them. It was a struggle'.

There is some evidence that systematic study patterns could be acquired. Avril, an accumulater, initially worked 'whenever I could snatch an hour' but later on when she needed a 'really organised phase', she filled out a study timetable and found she could adhere to it. Heena, who found studying 'very difficult to fit in with family life', also learned to focus quicker, to set herself a regular routine and do 'one little question at a time'. Holly had already perfected this skill. She liked to 'get everything out of the way, clear the decks and then settle down and do it'. She started 'from the word go', read independently, studied the tasks, planned ahead and, putting all the criteria on separate pieces of paper, collected together the evidence she needed. She often completed work well before the deadline.

Most of the women became adept at juggling home, work and study needs. Only a few students, like Ilsa, were able to command undisturbed study periods. Even at the end of the course, she remarked that: 'I have to have this huge bulk of time'. Ilsa called upon the support of visiting parents and would either take to the bedroom 'with the ironing board as a desk with my laptop on' or 'lose six to eight hours in the library'. Perhaps it was the availability of parents that allowed this trait to continue. Pregnant and with her husband on active service, studying offered respite from caring for an active toddler.

Overall, we see a variety of practices which show that for the majority, studying was a marginal activity they fitted around their family and work commitments.

Family support

Many students could only study undisturbed if they could delegate the child-care to someone else. In Ilsa's case it was her parents who supported her. A number of students could call upon their parents, suggesting an intergenerational interest in protecting the integrity of family, work and study. Evelyn, separated from her abusive husband, was living with her mother, seeking support after her breakdown. Alex relied on her mum to take children to school 'on college days'. Irene had a husband who 'understood how much time was required' but her young children disliked her 'going off to the office' so she developed a pattern of intensive working during the holidays, relying on grandparents as carers.

More commonly, students described partners who supported them, particularly by taking children out at weekends so that the student could study in peace. The husbands of Amy, Cindy, Daisy, Felicity, Frances, Faye, Gina and Heena were all prepared to do so. Daisy describes her husband, who works shifts, as 'domestic' and says he likes to cook. Heena's partner, despite giving psychological support, was 'not keen on housework' or on 'feeding everybody' and did not like it if 'there wasn't clean clothes to wear' but he did not mind if the 'house looked a complete pigsty', so when Heena had an assignment to write she knew exactly which jobs to prioritise and which to neglect. Bella's husband's business had just closed when she started both pre-school work and the Diploma course, so he was able to take care of their children. When her husband found a job, he scheduled his hours around the Diploma, so that 'his day off in the week became college day'. Bethany's husband also offered childcare initially as he was convalescent at home. Unfortunately, he required hospitalisation during the course, which 'did affect it a bit', but local family were able to help out. Bethany emphasises the positive aspects: 'It was quite trying ... but I was quite proud of myself really (laughs), how we managed, yes'. It is noticeable that all these situations reflect traditional gendered divisions within the family and that the women were grateful for any support offered rather than expecting it as a right.

Irma's husband offered her both emotional and practical support. Not only did he reassure her: 'you always think yourself thick or something ... but you're not', but he would sit up late into the night helping her edit excess words. 'We were up till 2 o'clock in the morning cutting them all out. He said, 'you've got to'.' Irma describes how she would ask him to read her assignment aloud so that she could hear 'if that sounds all right' and they would work on the grammar together. The husband continued critical support right through to the end, and he commented that her last assignment was 'so much different from the first one'. A close reading of this interview detects no hint of patronage or condescension in the support he gave her.

Other husbands were ambivalent or distinctly unhelpful, determined that studying should not intrude on family life. Deirdre claimed her husband thought she was just playing, Celia's husband made it a condition of study that 'you manage to get everything done here'. Consequently, she 'felt obliged to do everything else around the house'. These sentiments are echoed by Frieda, who states that, although 'he would probably deny it', her husband announced at the start of the course that it was 'fine as long as it doesn't affect me or the children'. So she had to 'scuttle around' 'fitting the college work around everything else'. Coping with these attitudes is very stress inducing. Celia describes crying over assignments 'many times over' at 'some ridiculous time of night'. Frieda claims that lack of support prevented her from going on to the foundation degree later.

> Certainly that went a long way to the decision not to go any further afterwards. Doing it to that level [3] was kind of the only space there was in my life at that time.

Sometimes children were supportive. Felicity acknowledges that her 'children were very good' when she studied but Ingrid's, admittedly older, children actually helped with her work. Ingrid describes how her two elder children 'sat there, sometimes until about 12 o'clock at night doing word counts for me and reading things through', allowing her to hear what she has written and to ask 'does that sound all right?' They also 'typed up notes for me' and 'did the hole-punching' during those 'few days before you are supposed to hand it in' when 'you just go completely off the rails'. By involving them, she not only got help but turned potential competition for her attention into a personal support system: a clever, if perhaps instinctive, strategy.

Sometimes support was a whole family affair, everyone recognising that 'mother' had needs – but this could be very small-scale. Cindy describes how 'the television never used to go on sometimes when I was writing the assignments'. For Emily it was the family allowing her to work on special occasions: 'one Boxing Day I did my coursework for the exams to hand in after Christmas', something she 'really enjoyed'. But she does not tell us what the rest of the family were doing.

A few of the students had no regular help. Heidi, mother of four, had to 'put the earplugs in and sit up in the bedroom and hope that no one is going to come barging through the door' but admitted she could not work 'when other people were in the house'. She also talked about 'fighting all the time' in her workplace, so she did well to complete at all: it was her third attempt. Danni also tried to 'lock myself away in the bedroom' after putting on 'a good video' for the children, because 'you can't farm them off to friends all the time'. An alternative was 'sending them for a long walk' with her husband, if he was not working away. He was prepared to do this although, she reluctantly admits, he was 'ambivalent' about her studying and, when I push harder, told me that 'he might not appreciate it' if she carried on 'beyond a degree'. After completing the Diploma, Danni had been one of the first to start, and also the first to stop, doing a foundation degree but she will only discuss this in terms of alternative choices: 'I knew for me to pass the course I would have needed to have given up everything else in my life and I felt that was asking too much'. For her, it would seem that a satisfactory family life and studying were not co-realisable options: her choices were constrained.

Avril, who had small children, talks about 'juggling everything around' but with difficulty: it was not 'a walk in the park'. Aileen says her husband 'never sort of mentioned it' and then adds 'we did our own thing – that's why we got divorced'. Alex, whose husband was neutral about her studying, explains that, although the course content was fine, it was hard to find the time:

> The two hours it is going to take to just sit down and think 'right this is what I am going to do, I'm not going to get any interruptions, the telephone isn't going to ring and there isn't going to be 'mum where's my tea', you know'.

Support comes in a range of forms: practical and emotional, involved and detached. Some of the support networks described here appear trivial: that someone allows you to work in the dining room, turns off the television, takes the children for a walk, cooks the occasional meal or does not complain if the house is a mess, do not appear in themselves to be very significant. That the students mention such things however, reveals just how important they are and just how difficult it is to study as an adult woman returner, when such minor inputs are vital and are the only help you get. The notable aspect of this support is that it is conditional: it is volunteered by partners, not demanded by students.

The situation varies between families but overall, linking these comments with the findings about patterns of working, it is clear that the students knew that they had to minimise the impact on the family of their studies. Partners could be supportive, or at least tolerant, but students were careful to monitor their own neediness and were acutely aware of the domestic chores that were essential to keep the peace within the family. This pattern suggests that within the family, Victorian values still apply and in many cases women's needs are secondary to those of the family. Paternal support is an option not a given, and even when freely offered, the help sometimes has a patronising feel.

Workplace issues

Although comments were not specifically sought, many students mentioned the levels of support at work, demonstrating again how the students integrated the different strands in their lives. Most found this satisfactory, if limited, often no more than being allowed time to carry out observations or activities, or giving a little moral support when the student was struggling with an assignment. The interviews capture the extreme viewpoints. Barbara, for example, found her setting very helpful. She enrolled with a more highly qualified colleague who 'would help me with my grammar which has *improved* considerably [and] correct my spellings'. And she 'could go and ask [the manager] about stuff', as 'she supports me'. In contrast, some groups were very unsympathetic, despite benefiting from the student's qualification. Bella's manager obstructed her learning. She said 'It would be 'well you can't do it today because so-and-so is not in', or 'I don't think we are going to have time because we have got a very busy morning'.' Holly, a volunteer in a group that rejected her ideas, was eventually forced to leave because 'they made my life an absolute misery'.

Students raised both generalised and specific complaints, and ultimately these determined whether the student would stay in the sector or later move on. Common protests related to excessive paperwork leading to more unpaid hours, moves to extend hours of opening that reduced the convenience benefits of working within the school day (as discussed in chapter 5), the pace of change itself and the difficulties of equating professionalism with voluntary management committees. Some students clearly derived great satisfaction from their jobs but in other cases, students described difficult conditions or atmospheres within a specific workplace.

Fuzzy work/life boundaries

Over the last decade there has been a significant increase in the requirement for childcare settings to produce business and curriculum plans, to document their meetings and decision-making processes and to monitor and record children's learning and achievements. These changes have been introduced in stages and many settings, operating on low levels of income, have been unable or unwilling to fully remunerate staff for such administrative duties. Some students undertook additional duties willingly, seeming to see this as commensurable with commitment and care. We saw how Evelyn enjoys going into work on a Sunday to help out: 'the reward isn't the pay'. Likewise, Bethany claims to 'get incredibly involved. Hours and hours I spend of my *own* time, doing things, it doesn't bear thinking about (laughs)'. Irma describes her colleague as 'working all weekends and missing out on family life'.

Felicity put in additional effort for a long time: 'there were lots of hours you were putting in, and I've never grumbled to the committee about that because I thoroughly enjoy what I do here'. She admits that 'you suddenly feel that's it, you've had enough' and decides that it is time to 'move on to the next stage'. Students appear to be prepared to work flexibly – but not forever. Heena was prepared to do additional paperwork at home until the expectations became too onerous. She explains how the increasing workload is invidious: 'we are asked to do it slowly and it builds up, that's what I found, it builds up, builds up builds up, until it's too much'.

Danni, too, allowed unpaid work commitments to flood into her private life. During the interview on her day off, she took a long phone call from the workplace to discuss the progress of a particular child who was causing concern. She is well aware of the insufficiency of her planning time: 'I get paid £20 something a week for administration', but recognises that 'in all fairness to the committee, they can't afford to pay more'. Failing to separate work and leisure cleanly can lead to exhaustion. She has already, at least temporarily, had to discontinue her foundation degree studies. Despite her dedication to the children and the group, she shows signs of tiring: 'sometimes you think, I would quite like to do something that doesn't need much preparation'. At another point in the interview however, she demonstrates that she is perfectly content to 'work' flexibly. She describes the Foundation Stage Forum website as 'a good way of getting the information you want in your own time'. Overall she seems more concerned to protect her part-time work status than to count the hours because when she talks about rates of pay, she says: 'if we get paid properly there will be a pressure on us to open all day'.

The practice of carrying out such tasks at home might be a continuation of the fuzzy boundary between volunteering and working and, within limits, the students are happy to do extra work at home. Many accept this as preferable to working longer hours, as that would detract from the convenience of the job in relation to their own children's needs. However, we see yet again that flexibility is bounded by family needs. If partners start to complain, students cut back commitments: greedy institutions check each other.

Excessive hours and paperwork

Early years workers tend to be naturally helpful people – which makes it easy to take advantage of them. Heena, for example, admits: 'I'm a yes person, you see. I don't like to upset anyone'. But her husband, although supportive of her work, asks 'why are you doing that, you are not getting paid for it' and it is his presence that reminds Heena to continually assess what she is taking on even if this is '*slightly* awkward'.

> I said 'give me the time and I will do it' because I thought 'how am I going to go home and tell my husband I m taking home all this extra work and I'm not going to get paid for it'.

Other husbands appear to behave in a similar manner – although there is always the possibility that students find it easier to project this attitude onto husbands in order to avoid any suggestion of personal selfishness. Beryl recalls her partner complaining 'you are doing more hours than I am working and you're getting a pittance'. Frieda's partner complains about the ratio of stress to remuneration:

> 'Okay, you have to be working but you don't have to be taking on board stress ... if it paid financially maybe it's worth having stress but if it doesn't it is very hard to justify'.

Similarly, Gina identifies 'a bit of grumbling, you know, at home': a partner who complains 'you do all this work and there's not much money coming in'.

For some students it is the paperwork itself that is perceived to be onerous. This is the reason why Greta is leaving the sector: 'I just feel it is drudgery now'. She complains about having to produce key activity plans and write up observations: similar concerns to those raised by Heidi, who 'just like[s] children to be children' and regrets that 'you've got to write down so much about what they can do'. Celia also dislikes the reporting requirement: 'can I just not do all this paperwork?'

Extended opening

Government policy has encouraged extended opening hours, and this is a source of concern as it undermines the *convenient* status of childcare work. Celia's group, in which she has worked for ten years, is opening a breakfast club and will 'eventually fulfil the government's wishes to do it till six o'clock at night', something that Celia does not intend to comply with.

> I'm not going down that road. Even when my children are that much older – my family comes first.

Ingrid is also concerned about plans for pre-schools to extend their opening hours, admitting that this does not suit her. 'I don't want to go to work 48 weeks of the year and put my own children in childcare for the sake of me going to work'. Danni expresses a concern for the children themselves, questioning whether longer sessions are in their best interests: 'By the time it gets to 12, I've got quite a number that are sitting there yawning and want to go home'.

Handling change

The students frequently discussed change and keeping up to date, and their attitudes varied across a continuum from apathy to enthusiasm. Certain students felt that 'others' should update them. Arianne, for instance, is concerned that the ground rules alter and training becomes 'obsolete' and she finds it 'hard to keep up with the change'. Ingrid echoes this complaint: 'I feel we are quite let down when it comes to keeping us in touch with things that change'. Few students feel as strongly as Celia, who can no longer tolerate the pace of change.

> I *find* the constant change of demands by the government and the powers that be ... *utterly* frustrating.

Many groups rely on successive students feeding back new ideas. Frieda, for instance, explains that: 'we have [staff member] doing level 3 currently so we will be keeping up to date for as long as she is doing that'. Avril also mentions asking current students to let her know 'if anything new comes through' and jests that 'you need some kind of outside trainer whose job it is to keep up' but, like Bethany, she relies upon courses, magazines and the internet. For them, as for many others, the cluster meetings and short courses provided by the county training service are held at inconvenient times. Some, like Irene, find them useful but many find they do not fit in with busy lives. Danni says they have often 'clashed with something else that has been a higher priority really'. Ingrid claims that they are 'either too far away or the days are wrong'.

One of the advantages of moving into a school setting is that the responsibility for updating is taken away. Beryl describes how new ideas 'are fed down to us really' and accepts the limitations of this process: 'You only get bits, only hear what you have to do, you don't often hear the whys and wherefores and where it's coming from'. Where there are supernumerary managers in pre-schools, students show similar patterns of dependence. Barbara, Emily, Cindy and Gina are content to rely upon managers to disseminate new information. A few students embrace change enthusiastically, like Holly, who believes that if 'you want to be abreast of things then you will go and do and keep ahead of the game anyway'. Danni's reaction is more typical: 'you can see that major, major changes are coming up again. Do you want to go through another major change? Or ...?'

Problems in the workplace

Discussions about the workplace demonstrate its semi-voluntary status and perhaps explain how students are able to continue to mix work and family commitments in an *ad hoc* way. Pre-schools are generally all-female establishments, run by voluntary committees, and, as Heena jokes, subject to that 'time of the month when everybody's (...) at the same time, completely stressed, but you keep your head down'. Amy, we have already heard, changed jobs when her playgroup committee challenged the supervisors' ways of working. Holly also had to leave her group because of poor staff relationships and Evelyn describes the stresses of working with a new playleader who 'knew where she was going in her career' and 'didn't mind who she stepped over to get to it'. This conflict-ridden working environment distressed Evelyn, making her 'physically sick before I went to work'.

Celia finds her manager difficult to work with: 'it's just the injustice year on year, upsetting people, saying nasty things about people'. She claims to be fond of the supervisor but the situation is volatile – there is 'slamming doors and unpleasantness' – and workers carry out health and safety procedures clandestinely rather than confronting the manager with problems that anger her. Perhaps feeling a little disloyal, Celia then adds that the parents with whom she works drive her 'bonkers' too. 'I find I am just worn out of watching children *tell their* ... 2-year-old children tell their parents what they are going to do, when and where and how.'

Nor are breaches of health and safety codes and professionalism confined to the voluntary sector. Working in a day nursery, Imogen described a period of non-observance of staffing ratios; shortages of cleaning materials, sanitiser and gloves, and having no cleaner for two weeks; staff being bullied and children teased rather than comforted when they were upset. The nursery owners became aware that there were problems, dismissed some staff and sent in a temporary manager to implement improvements, but Imogen saw new difficulties arising out of these reforms.

The maintained sector is not exempt from problems. Beryl, working in a nursery class, finds the early years curriculum distorted as 'the school ideas are coming right the way down'. She describes having to introduce 3-year-olds to the school's success criteria – the 5Rs – of which *she* can only re-member resilience, resourcefulness and responsibility; excessive planning and paperwork; termly parental consultations; zero absenteeism despite schooling being non-compulsory; and structured days revolving around allocated slots for the ICT suite, the hall and the playground. It is 'like they forgot that these children are pre-school'. She is also surprised that the school employs someone trained for an older age group as early years co-ordinator, a practice that is not uncommon.

Committees

Committees were mentioned less often than I expected. Heidi and Irene encountered specific problems with their committees and Danni described the irritation caused by inconsistent behaviour from one year to the next: 'we can't reinvent the wheel every year, you know'. Bethany echoed this concern, describing the voluntary management committee as 'the ultimate worst thing'.

> Every year you have a new employer ... every committee comes on and every couple of years people have totally different ideas as to what the priorities should be.

Frieda too is perturbed that 'my employer who can advise me on how to run my playgroup is unqualified, untrained, a very well-meaning, very well-intentioned mum' and would like 'to have a professional advising me and for me to be reporting to a professional'. She does not think that the government strategy of sending in advisers who 'kind of dip in and then dip out' makes up for the committee's inadequacies.

That there were only five negative comments among a cohort of 33 students suggests that most of the trained staff are coping with this management structure. Committees are perhaps becoming more professional than they once were or are now better supported by advisers and trainers – mostly the students in the interview sample were working in groups that were still committee run.

The educational context

Before considering the students' views of educational practices it is useful to look at strategies common to adult education. There is a significant body of work investigating how to make provision more user friendly, much of which the FE college has tried to implement.

Addressing barriers to education

It is well established that women returning to education encounter a range of problems. This, and possible solutions, were thoroughly researched in the 1990s by Veronica McGivney (1993) and Maggie Coats (1994) among others. Some problems are practical: finance, transport, childcare; some are familial: partner disapproval, caring commitments to sick children and elderly parents; some are personal: lack of confidence, lack of study skills, and poor health, physical or mental, after being housebound for years. At national level, childcare is seen as a strategic priority so for some time fees have been paid, at least in part, through the European Social Fund or other national initiatives.

Within the FE college, a number of exceptional practices facilitated integration of family and workplace needs. Mobile phones could be left on, course hours, teaching breaks and coursework deadlines respected school attendance patterns and so did study, counselling and other support services. Priority timetabling provided students with a single base room for the entire day and the normal rules about eating and drinking in teaching rooms were waived to allow more flexible working. As course tutor, I took responsibility for all aspects of the course – recruitment, enrolment, teaching, assessment and feedback – so the students received clear messages about expectations. A large number of concessions were made, many of which had to be renegotiated through successive college restructurings. When I asked students if college met their needs as adults, I was trying to monitor whether these concessions were consciously recognised, irrelevant or simply taken for granted.

The majority of students felt that their needs *were* met but said little about *how*. Aileen and Alex mentioned that for them one-day-a-week attendance was important, and several said that the delayed start was good as it allowed them to take their children to school first. Being able to park was significant, as without that facility the advantages of a 10 am start disappeared. Only two preferred cycling to college and several came by bus, complaining about the inefficient routes. Freedom to use the library for independent study was mentioned by Arianne and for some students food was important, especially when students travelled together and saw the course as a 'day out'. Aileen talks of meeting up with Alex and going to buy pizza before college, Arianne of stopping at Tesco's with Alice to get 'something naughty'. Later in the interview she says that having coffee and 'biscuits on the table' and the chance to chat were vital. For the two students coping with agoraphobia, having a single room and a stable environment was essential. Holly pointed out how her 'little regime' gave her security: 'I stayed in to dinner, brought my own lunch with me and I didn't leave the classroom unless it was to use the toilet'. Similarly, Heena relied on a set routine, arriving early: 'Just to make sure I was here, to make sure nothing had gone wrong'.

The discussion of supportive educational arrangements – although limited – is useful, as it demonstrates that the concessions are truly necessary 'hygiene' factors (cc) rather than optional 'motivational' ones (Herzberg, 1959). Given that the rate of pre-school pay was so low, fee support was also an essential hygiene factor but I have no way of establishing this. Most students had their fees paid in full by the local authority: in the research period, childcare students experienced a fortuitous synchrony between their personal desire to train and the government bid to extend provision and also raise standards in the sector. Only three students (Holly, Hansa and Ilsa) talked about funding the course themselves, and a further five students, working as volunteers, were given 50 per cent funding (Daisy, Gina, Heena, Irene, Irma). Deirdre used working tax credits to pay for the course, and two others, on benefits, were able to attend for free.

Holly chose independence and Hansa had 'no time to think'. She only became eligible for fee support when she met the residential requirements so was forced to juggle one day in college, six hours voluntary work in a pre-school setting, study time and a 40-hour shop job in order to support her student partner. Consequently, Ilsa was the only student who monitored value for money and I noted that she fretted if other students distracted me and *she* felt that we had not 'covered the criteria that we needed to cover today'.

Of particular interest is Gina's attitude. She felt a bit of a 'pretender' in the group. For her degree course, also undertaken as a mature student, she had been intensively interviewed and requested to submit essays to demonstrate her competence. The selection process boosted her confidence: 'they have chosen me because I am able to do this'. To be allowed onto the Diploma without pre-assessment left Gina insecure and doubtful about her ability. This demonstrates in an unanticipated way how educational practices can encourage dependence, even when the intervention is not of a therapeutic nature.

Students freely commented on educational practices within the classroom, how they experienced different types of assessment and their preferred teaching styles. This offered insights into the transformational aspect of education: its role in the development of capability rather than as a capability in its own right.

Approaches to assignments

I was interested to discover how assessment practices support student development and in particular the usefulness of criteria. Making sense of the guidance and criteria always takes a great deal of time in class and students complain about the obtuse nature and ambiguity of the wording. Very few students approach assignment criteria with the rigour shown by Holly:

> I used to go E1, 2, 3, 4, 5, 6, 7 and 8 and A, B, C, D, and make a heading on a piece of paper and putting my thought on that piece of paper right from the word go.

Therefore, when I encouraged interviewees to consider task definitions I was surprised to find the majority, particularly cohort 'F', in favour of structure – in hindsight at least. Perhaps the contradictory behaviour is typical. Aileen admits:

> It was set out really well. I mean, I know I complained bitterly through most of the course but it was quite easy to do and work through.

What is noticeable is the number of times students refer to the tutor function of assisting with interpretation of criteria. Arianne, Cindy, Danni, Emily, Heena, Heidi and Ilsa all did so, suggesting they had some difficulty with the process. Danni, a motivated and intelligent student, claimed that 'I don't think I could have done it without the support'. However, there is evidence that understanding how to write to criteria is a learnable process and several students (Evelyn, Greta, Ilsa and Hansa) talked positively of gaining the confidence to do it alone.

For Heena the criteria set limits to the task. She claims that a simple essay title only tells you 'where to start' but not where to 'stop'. Although she found 'the slight difference' in wording between hierarchical criteria difficult, she was reassured by the knowledge that if she met all the criteria she had answered the question whereas with a 'big heading' she would have just kept on writing.

> It's how far do you go – and if you've written all this stuff – have you covered what the examiner is possibly looking for?

Ingrid liked to have 'rules, or whatever you would like to call them, to actually adhere to and to work to'. Heidi also recognised the value of criteria 'because if you just had the titles you could go off in any direction' but was critical of 'the way they word it sometimes'. Emily was alone among the non-graduates in preferring a more open type of essay but her reasons had more to do with autonomy than academy. She found the criteria 'very grey' and did not want to 'keep bothering people' for help.

I was particularly interested in the responses of the graduates as they were accustomed to writing essays. Irene found the criteria prescriptive, as did Daisy for whom they were also an irritant as they forced her to focus. Dianne was neutral, seeing a degree and a vocational course as entirely different. Gina and Greta saw them as both 'helpful' and 'restrictive': on the one hand they specified content, on the other they were hard to interpret. Gina blithely used them as a checklist but Greta struggled with their specificity as it underlined the possibility of failure. Only Irene suggested that criterion-based assessment was less challenging, realising after completing one assignment that there was no point editing her work to 'make it flowing and well-structured' as this would not seriously increase her marks.

These findings neither fully support nor devalue criterion-based assessment. I was at first surprised that so many students who had complained about the issue of criteria at the time favoured them retrospectively, but this instrumental attitude can probably be explained by time constraints. The criteria allowed students to complete work piecemeal. Once grasped, they minimised the individual effort required to write an assignment. So viewed, criteria become an important asset in the juggling of family, work and study time. What the research also highlights, however, is that criteria represent an additional stage in the planning and writing processes and this is helpful for those who are unsure when to stop and start and restrictive for those with greater capabilities. Thus, criteria do suit the less able student and may have a place in vocational practice but not in higher education. However, to be truly useful they need to be clearly written to support autonomous learning and obviate the need for tutor interpretation.

Views on course structures

It is this individualised support that matters to many students. All the students on the diploma had clearly chosen a taught course but some compared this route to distance learning and National Vocational Qualifications (NVQs) and this sheds light on their values. Two issues seem to be important here. One concerns student isolation and tutor support, the 'nightmare' of only seeing tutors once a month, compared to the Diploma where, as Avril claims: 'you met each other often enough to build up a relationship'. The second is standards-related: the fear that NVQs restrict learning as they endorse current workplace practices rather than encouraging improvement. In capability terms, the original aim of an NVQ is to accredit an existing functioning, whereas a taught course sets out to expand capability.

Ingrid completed a college-based level 2 NVQ six months before signing up for the Diploma, so can make a personal comparison. She mentions 'struggling' with the first Diploma assignment, as she lacked confidence and was unused to writing things and setting things out and thinking about 'the words to use'. For the NVQ – a paper-free trial – she had merely had to 'write little sentences in the box' whereas for the Diploma she had to write three thousand word reports. Ingrid found the tutor support was vital: 'If you had just chucked it at us and said 'you have to do this' then I would have probably gone completely off my head'. Once Ingrid had made the adjustment, however, she did enjoy the taught course, valuing group support.

> Oh I much preferred to actually be able to come somewhere and see somebody and work with people.

Bella also thought that college attendance was important, making the point that the co-operation learned face-to-face with other group members assists the development of the personal skills needed to manage an early years setting, the ability to listen and to work as a team: 'you need to have the skills to get on with people'. Here she is describing the 'soft skills' currently in demand in the workplace notwithstanding the emphasis on formal qualifications; skills that are often developed through daily contact within the family and local community.

Learning and teaching preferences

About half the students commented on teaching and learning styles, and the female epistemological framework proposed by Belenky, Clinch, Goldberger and Tarule (1997/86, cc women's ways of knowing) proved to be a useful analytical support. This research classifies women's learning approaches into five hierarchical categories. The *silenced* conform wordlessly, their sense of self damaged by ill-treatment. The *receivers* learn passively, wanting teachers to provide a single universal 'truth'. The *subjective* seek a personal understanding but rely heavily on intuition. The *procedural* are mechanically acquiring the skills of academic discourse. Only the *constructors* operate subjectively and objectively, viewing knowledge as contextual.

I believe that some students found my teaching style difficult because they were still working at the received level. They wanted facts transmitted, saw the teacher as a source of authority, wanted predictability and clarity and therefore favoured the maths and sciences. They sought one right answer for a problem, disliked debate and ambiguity, and were loath to apply material. Four students (Arianne, Greta, Heena and Heidi) made it clear that they liked to be taught rather than sent out to find things out for themselves. Arianne, Barbara and Deirdre also said that they liked the teaching day to be structured but further analysis revealed that they meant different things by this phrase. Arianne, whom I found more flexible, liked her study 'chopped up into workable loads' and wanted to be 'kept on the ball' but also to be given breaks for 'coffee and biscuits' and 'a little chat among us', whereas Barbara and Deirdre wanted a much more linear approach. Barbara admits to finding it 'hard sometimes to follow my strand'. She liked the sciences and practical work, but said she still finds the flexibility of 'working as a team' difficult. Only now, as a foundation degree student around a decade later, is she beginning to enjoy debates.

Deirdre disliked it if I deviated from the syllabus and later admitted to being irritated by any meetings or courses that strayed outside her interest zone. For her, studying was only ever 'to get on' in her career. Ilsa, the armed forces officer, also liked science and active learning: 'I've got a very short attention span unless I am doing something practical'. She liked the course to follow the syllabus precisely and regarded student discussion as a diversion. These students were all in the received knowledge category, although Arianne was showing signs of moving on a stage. My style of teaching, which was about encouraging exploration of ideas, was intended to develop their capacity to think independently, and this was sometimes contested. Balancing the different demands of the student group was quite challenging, requiring me, as tutor, to enforce elements of compromise at times.

A few students were changing their learning style during the Diploma, moving into the subjective category and finding their own perspectives. Fiona, as well as liking science and structured approaches, valued in-depth learning and enjoyed conceptual ideas like schemas (cc) and the spiral curriculum (cc). Greta, although a graduate, wanted transmission, access to 'knowledge built on your past experience' and disliked tangential ideas. But she did recognise that 'it's a good reflection on you that people feel confident that they can ask' things and saw that 'their experience and advice you gave them could help with problems we had too'. So she was beginning to see the value of shared opinions, and was possibly moving towards the 'anecdotal' transmission of knowledge favoured by Heena, Heidi, Frances and Cindy, as it made learning memorable.

Indeed, Heidi believed 'access to other people's experiences' to be 'a better way of learning'. So did Heena, who thought 'having the other people in similar situations and all those class discussion was fabulous'. Frances, unable yet to synthesise material and very focused on self-analysis, was typically located in the subjective zone. I feel that Imogen too, a bright girl who had A-levels, had the ability to enter debate but not yet the confidence to speak out. For instance, she acknowledges that 'you taught me some things' but her insight that at other times 'you were helping me remember what I knew' is a lay description of drawing out prior learning. This demonstrates a degree of sensitivity that is lost when she echoes the views of less reflective student friends.

Those students who favoured discursive learning – Felicity and Frieda for example – were possibly straddling the boundary between subjective and procedural learning, as they appealed to reason in their debates and were able to avoid taking issues personally. Felicity foregrounds the debates as 'really interesting', enabling her to 'pick up other ideas' and think 'how you might deal with something' and is excited when 'stories come out'. Frieda, recognising that in-depth learning matters more than meeting criteria, sums up the issues of debates and tangents perfectly. When asked what made an impact she demonstrated a sophisticated ability to self-reflect:

> The level of discussion we used to have ... it would have been quite easy just to learn how to answer the questions ... but thinking ... in a much more rounded way meant that I learned much more than just how to pass the assignment.

It is probable that other students who failed to comment on pedagogic practices were also operating at this level. Being flexible learners, they would have been able to cope with a range of teaching practices without being adversely affected. Exceptionally, Daisy (the graduate whose aspirations were curtailed by a head injury) demonstrates an aspect of the highest category of learning, the constructor. Not content with the common breakdown of learning into areas remembered through the acronym SPICE (social, physical, intellectual, communicative and emotional), she adds another E for environment as she believes that to be important.

Irma was possibly the student who travelled the greatest social distance during the Diploma course but this was because she started at such a low level. Her focus was the practicalities of studying, possibly having been 'silenced' during her schooldays by her difficult childhood. From her comments, I would deduce that she had moved from a non-learner to a receiver of knowledge, focusing particularly on the processes of studying and formulating these as rules of behaviour. She mentioned the processes of note-taking and her acquisition of knowledge about assignments, bibliographies and computer file management but also on how to comport herself in a classroom.

She claimed confidently that: 'I can do any course now, I know I could do it, just sit and listen, write everything down – fine.'

Belenky and colleagues' levels (1997/86) offer a useful interpretation of students' apparent study preferences. The tenacity with which the students at the lower level argued the case for knowledge transmission suggests that they were unable rather than unwilling to consider alternative approaches. However, the seemingly instrumental preference for straightforward teaching that contradicts philosophical preferences for a liberal education might also reflect the need to manage busy lives and conflicting needs. Student decision-making is essentially pragmatic, integrated lives have to work. If you have very little time to study, and need basic knowledge in the workplace, discussion of broader issues may seem a luxury. Greta's views epitomise this desire to stay focused and, as a graduate and very reflective person she could never be categorised as incapable of studying beyond receiver level. Before moving on to discuss educational consequences, we should note her enthusiasm for learning:

> I was willing to learn so I would have been happy to listen to anything ... when I felt things had gone off on a tangent ... I felt we had lost time ... I'm here, this is a valuable day.

This chapter reveals the importance of physical and social structures in education. Qualities that were repeatedly claimed to be valuable were being in a class with similar people and face-to-face contact with tutors. Also important were appropriate settings in terms of hours, convenience and cost but these attracted less comment – probably because suitable conditions were already embedded. The central focus of this chapter is the balancing of competing demands and there appeared to be two main ways this could be achieved: through fuzziness and fragmentation.

Fuzziness is seen in the ways that boundaries were blurred and practices overlapped: the ways the students took paperwork home, fitted studying around the housework, and left college work out permanently to grab the precious moments when the children were out, asleep or otherwise occupied. Night-time study was rare, however, as children came first and sleepy parents could not cope with caring.

Fragmentation is evident in the approval for assessment criteria that divided assignments into composite tasks and the practice of studying episodically. For some, study patterns were chaotic, as the student snatched random moments between other tasks. Others planned carefully, allocating specific tasks to anticipated opportunities, and there is some evidence that this organisational skill could be acquired.

Whichever approach a student favoured, all valued time in college and this created a preference for knowledge transmission, as they deemed it to be efficient. By these and other means the students were balancing competing demands and doing so with good humour. They would have liked more time to do things properly but not if this meant narrowing their options, so they were exercising choice as they strived to integrate their lives.

By building on our knowledge of expectations and practices, the next chapter looks at the consequences of studying in order to complete the chronological analysis. It links specific detail and holistic overview to develop understanding of the role of education in integrating lives.

7

Considering the consequences of studying

This chapter analyses the changes the students ascribe to their educational experience as adults, in light of the expectations and practices within education. The analysis uses both the internalised long-term reflections recalled during the interviews, and the more recent evaluations prompted by the shared interview process. Despite the vocational nature of the Diploma course, the consequences of studying include significant personal gains. These are – somewhat arbitrarily – divided into the individual and the social in the students' accounts. Other consequences more clearly relate to the family, the workplace and education itself and the transferable and transformational nature of the learning emerges. Taking a longitudinal approach makes such connections apparent. A survey across the students' biographies demonstrates how, when integrating their lives, they utilise any prior experiences that fit their current purposes. As we saw in chapter 4, choices for many mature women are compound, with new functionings deriving from previous successful capability conversion.

Individual gains

The consequence most often identified in the interviews was confidence. More than 50 per cent of the students named this attribute but closer analysis reveals that each student used the term differently. Although a psychological attribute for everyone, confidence can relate to inner feelings in isolation or to the ability to do something new, different or simply better. Thus it has two major facets – the internal and the external – but often these are linked in a specific activity, as in Evelyn's comment that the Diploma 'gave me the *confidence* to go into the school', a sentiment echoed by Frances.

For Faye the sense of confidence is internalised. She had struggled all through secondary school to express herself on paper. Detailed probing revealed that she was still unsure 'whether I had learning difficulties or not'. Qualifying for work purposes was important to Faye but even greater was the need 'to do it to prove to myself perhaps that I could do it'. She needed to feel educated and to 'put a line under' her past sense of inadequacy. Fiona felt she now had some academic competence, that she could write essays and 'get the grades'. Irma felt much the same. She had had no previous contact with educational procedures but says: 'I can do any course now'.

Heena also claims that confidence was her 'main thing' and believed she 'had the knowledge to back it up' when making decisions in the group. She also acquired study skills 'because I had never written essays before' although she had a higher national diploma in computing. She believes that 'having that education really does help'. In the past she was terrified of forms and admits to 'sort of avoiding' them. That forms are among the 'things I can now face' sounds really positive because avoidance is one of the traits which underpins agoraphobia, and Heena suffers from this.

> It's kind of really nice to be good at something *and* being able to develop that. I think it's huge for self-esteem, especially if you enjoy it.

Heidi, whose interview also suggests some unresolved issues, developed the confidence to make changes in her setting. She talks at length about setting up a snack bar that 'went down really, really well'. She had worked at the pre-school for thirteen years before qualifying so it was rather surprising to learn that only now is she confident talking to parents: 'if you speak to them and be yourself instead of trying to be somebody else you actually do get on with them quite well'. Heidi claims she has newly acquired the confidence to discipline children with a 'look', and it is reassuring to hear that the course has made her 'more of a calmer person' and taught her that 'shouting at them doesn't get you anywhere'. Heidi's examples of growing confidence demonstrate the interrelated consequences of the course. In one short paragraph she has mentioned a workplace change, social development, and growing competence when dealing with children – all developments relevant to vocational practice but seen by the student as personal changes.

Even students who were already competent talk about their confidence. Gina, a humanities graduate, felt insecure about approaching a vocational qualification and speaks of developing the 'confidence ... to be able to, to do something and do it well'. Greta, a history graduate, gained confidence by qualifying, as 'there is a thread running through me of not completing things'. She clearly used her learning to validate her own beliefs: 'I felt I could challenge because it wasn't just my inner neurosis or inner rage or whatever'. For Imogen the confidence came from 'making new friends', learning about children, and giving feedback to parents: 'I know how to say things – how to word it'. Cindy too lists confidence to deal with parents, adding 'especially if they have different cultures or religions'. In admitting that 'before, you would probably be too scared to do things like that', she is expressing the popular belief that prejudice grows out of fear and that education can alleviate it. And Ingrid describes how the course gave her 'much more confidence in looking at people as just people' and specifically describes a practical activity she carried out which widened her own and her group's understanding of the Holi festival. By working closely with a Hindu family to celebrate this event, she extended her understanding of their culture and seems able to project this newfound tolerance onto people generally. She describes herself as a 'lot nicer person' and believes she is a 'lot less judgemental now'.

> People outside, I think, of my general circle of friends and family, I now feel as though I could go and speak to confidently whereas I would probably just have passed them by in the street before.

Although classed as personal developments, many of these consequences have a bearing on the social domain and, in application, on vocational practice, thus demonstrating the holistic nature of such changes. However, the changes are centred within the individual, whereas those in the social domain have a broader shared significance. Status – a key consequence for two students, though less important to others – appears to straddle the boundary between the personal and social, being an individualised trait and dependent on the respect of others. Danni, for instance, clearly enjoys the pre-school's close connections to the local primary. She describes a friendly relationship with the headteacher and how he sends in his new reception teacher, who is 'really struggling', 'just to see what we do and to see how we operate'. This is good for the playleader's self-esteem and so are the accolades from parents whose children also attend the local, and significantly more expensive, day nursery, who say: 'Oh they enjoy coming to you much more than they enjoy going to day nursery'. Unlike staff in a commercial venture, the pre-school supervisor merely settles down to work even harder to maintain the difference, rather than raising charges, demonstrating again that the reward is personal satisfaction or community support, not financial gain. Bethany is another who presents a strong picture of someone who works for status rather than salary. She derives immense satisfaction from her work:

'I have made a *damn good successful* playgroup'. She is highly motivated by reactions from other people, particularly the local primary headteacher.

Social gains

Work on social capital suggests that one of the key benefits of education is likely to be a strengthening of community ties but in my localised research I found only limited evidence of the students developing lasting relationships. There are several possible explanations for this situation. The relatively low status and high demands of childcare work could mean that students have few benefits to share. Their skills lie in areas like emotional support and practical care, areas that attract little public attention. Possibly their underpaid and undervalued work in the early years settings is in itself their contribution to the community and leaves them little inclination to make further links. Beryl talks about running the Brownies, Irene is involved with the Rainbows and Bethany sees being a parent governor as an extension to running the village pre-school.

Amongst the study cohort, Ingrid is unusual in that she used her newfound confidence to take on a further community role – as a parent governor at the local school, which she 'would never have *dreamed* of doing before'. Conversely, greater awareness can actually discourage volunteering. Ingrid thinks that 'what is expected of volunteer parents is too much' and she 'would have to think twice about becoming a chair or treasurer voluntary again'. Bella now deems the local parent staff association guilty of 'a lot of pontification and maybe not enough action' and wants to avoid 'all that rubbish' in future.

The students appear to be able to settle onto the course quite quickly but not necessarily to form lasting friendships and we saw in chapter 4 how social capital bonding and bridging can explain this pattern. Certainly, I found little evidence that students stayed in touch with each other when the Diploma finished. Exceptionally, within the study cohort, Arianne still occasionally meets up with Alice, Holly describes a continuing friendship with Harriet, and Hansa has kept in touch with Hebe. Ingrid explains that she got 'quite close' to Iva but is realistic in expecting that contact with others will be slight.

> I made some really good friends and they were a great bunch of girls but I think we have now gone off and we will do our own things in our own lifetime and we will probably hear from each other now and again.

There is evidence that students who worked together cemented their existing friendships by travelling and studying together. For example, Felicity and Frieda deliberately studied together knowing they were to become joint play-leaders, and several similar pairs stayed in touch. Bethany and Cindy kept in touch with 'friends' for a time but then gradually drifted apart. Most of the students share Aileen's view that 'life takes over'. This 'moving on' is even true of the cohort 'F', who socialised as a group. Frances lists nine other students with whom she had 'met up' on several occasions but when asked whom she still contacts, can mention only one student, Fanny, whom she sees 'very occasionally'. Like many other students she is just too busy to maintain deliberate contact. As Cindy observes, 'once you work full-time you are limited on time'. Generally, the interviews generate a feeling of casual warmth towards the majority of fellow students, typified by Irma's comment:

> I haven't made a point of seeing them again. I've got their emails and that but if I see 'em in the street I would definitely go and talk to them.

There is plentiful evidence of casual encounters. Many students talk of meeting others in supermarkets or being pleased to see familiar faces at cluster meetings and at short courses in the county. From my own experience of tracing almost the entire cohort I know that many of the students know of the whereabouts of others even if they rarely contact them. This should not be unexpected for, as Evelyn explains, many people fail to contact friends on a regular basis. *Social meshing* usefully describes the interactional benefits of the Diploma course: they serve a cohesive role, filling interstices in the social fabric rather than creating it. However, this is a form of social capital and is significant in creating a sense of belonging to the childcare community. Felicity demonstrates this sense of connection well in the following extract.

> Occasionally I bump into people on courses still. It's nice to see them as well ... I've kept in touch with Fanny initially and I've seen her – I saw her just before Christmas. I bumped into her in a shop and we hope to get together, all of us, soon. She keeps in touch with Frances, that's nice, and obviously I met Faith again doing the foundation degree because we were on the same day so I saw her. There are one or two scattered about – Flora's a good friend of Georgia and I hear what Flora is up to from Georgia from time to time.

Effects on family

Holly saw the Diploma as benefiting her family as well as her employment prospects: 'if I learn all this I can transfer it to my children'. This relating of learning to their own family is likely with a childcare course and is mentioned specifically by a number of students, often in relation to problems they have or had with specific children. Avril 'really wished that I had had that information when they were younger' and admits that now they are teenagers she is 'totally lost again'. Celia similarly recalls saying out loud: 'I wish I'd known that when [son] was 2 years old' and ensures she relays her knowledge to other parents whose children she cares for, recognising the importance of 'just saying to mums that it's okay, that's normal'. Emily too is sure that the knowledge helped with her son 'even though he was older than the range we were studying'. She also gains self-esteem indirectly by being able to pass on child-development knowledge to others: 'they wanted to know what was normal at what age'. Irene, already a graduate, believes that 'it's given me more understanding of what my children are doing – my own children'. She recognises that she has mastered the necessary jargon, and has tackled her children's headteacher about self-esteem issues 'which I probably wouldn't have done if I hadn't have had this training'. Ilsa takes pleasure in advising her sister-in-law on what to do when her youngest will not settle at nursery and describes a '*huge* sense of satisfaction' from completing the Diploma, believing that 'working with children has calmed me down' and 'it helped me with my own child'.

For Alex the knowledge from the Diploma has even come in useful when dealing with a teenager at secondary school: 'Because now I know if I push and I push and I push I am going to get somewhere'. Celia however was less brave. For her the course 'certainly did awaken in me an understanding of why my son struggled so badly through primary school' but 'I didn't do anything about it'. Her son hated drawing, his manipulative skills were poorly developed, and he attended a school where most aspects of reading and writing were taught through this medium. He quickly earned the label 'very untidy' from a teacher, who scrawled this in red ink over his work within his first few weeks. Celia hated to see her 4-year-old 'miserable, miserable' but felt it was 'pointless to try to challenge the whole system at the school'. Consequently she sees herself in a negative light: 'I'm frightened of the teachers, I'm that sort of coward'. In this instance, it is hard to say whether the greater understanding helped or hindered the family.

On one occasion a student, Frieda, talks about 'a huge period of guilt' when her learning caused her to believe that some of her son's emotional problems can be attributed 'to the way I handled him as a toddler probably'. She is highlighting the painful, perhaps even negative, consequences of learning about children after having already had your own. But she recognises that she might not have taken the material 'as seriously had I done it before' and acknowledges that it did help her to change 'the way I talked to them', and to develop 'more realistic' expectations. So the experience was probably positive overall. The confidence to work with parents, the self-esteem from having a professional qualification and knowing how to find things out for the future ('I knew where to go, to the books, to the resources to find more information') are all additional benefits for Frieda to offset against the guilt.

Vocational adjustments

The vocational consequences of studying were surprisingly sparse, at least in the short term. Most stayed in similar or slightly better jobs, indicating that the training was to maintain the *status quo* rather than to achieve change. A number of students (13 of the 33) tried to, or actually did, change jobs during the year when data was collected but 23 students continued to work in early years settings during the research period (18 in the PVI sector, 5 as TAs in primary schools). A further four considered themselves to be working in related fields (play specialist, early years educator, paediatric nurse, and agency staff). Frances, who combined her previously acquired administrative skills with her interest in children to work in a secondary school, also saw clear lines of continuity between her two jobs but, for classificatory purposes, her work has taken her out of child*care* as her contact is now with older children and incidental to the role of arts co-ordinator. So altogether only six students were no longer directly involved in the sector, and two of those were on maternity leave.

Most people continued to work in childcare. In Holly's terms, they were 'stuck in this rut'. In Sen's terms, they were choosing functioning from within their capability set. The element of choice, however, was very important. As Arianne explicitly states, she decided to stay in her setting but was pleased that the Diploma gave her the 'option to leave'. She has a qualification that is transferable, should she want to move on.

Stepping up

Chapter 3 introduced the concept of a step-upper, a student who has moved into a significantly better job, and cited Fiona as a representative. Fiona's decision to train to be a nurse was largely children-oriented but on a personal level she wanted and gained a proper career, stable employment and a fair wage. She sees the Diploma course as a significant factor underpinning her new career path. It was important in terms of skill development and outlook: 'You taught us how to write an essay and I realised that I still had it in me, and that sort of flourished so to speak, went into flower'. This allowed her access to a nursing degree so the Diploma gave Fiona more than the basic knowledge of child development, child protection and knowing how to work with parents – skills she acknowledges that she still uses.

Amy went from joint playleader, via a short time as a hospital crèche worker, to a play specialist after completing a second training course. She traced her interest in hospital work to the Diploma and how it motivated her also to enrol on a word-processing course. 'When we went and visited the wards on the course, I thought, oh that looks an interesting job'. Thus, in her case, the Diploma awakened an interest in continuing education and a new career which gave access to a 'normal' wage.

Another step-upper is Avril, who saw the Diploma as the first fundamental step in the many she took to reach her post of adult educator.

> When I first went into the [Diploma] I was like stretched because I hadn't studied for a long time ... and you never know it might give me the edge not to take things for granted and to try a bit harder.

Bella saw the Diploma as important to her because 'it made sense of the job', and this in turn made her 'confident in what I do do'. She has moved from pre-school, to running her own afternoon sessions as a business, to being head-teacher of a private nursery school where she will earn 'two and a half times what I was earning'.

> It is a proper job – it's got, you know, nine weeks paid holiday, um, a pension ... They are going to want a lot for their money but it's at a level I would never have achieved'.

At interview, Felicity says she is looking forward slightly nervously to her new, salaried, advisory role. She knows she will in future be paid for holidays and for the hours worked, whereas in the pre-school situation 'I quite often do a four and a half – five hour day – and get paid for three'. Having just completed a foundation degree, she claims that the panel 'were very impressed with it' and the transferable skill element had led to a successful interview. Felicity states that the Diploma motivated her to enrol on the degree course, so traces a clear career path which originated in the Diploma.

> I had really enjoyed doing this Diploma and I was pleased with my results ... and I wanted to do something else, wanted to do that little bit more.

Other students have taken on a more managerial role within childcare. Cindy 'moved on to another nursery' in search of longer hours and greater respon-sibility before gaining a post in another county as a nursery manager. Arianne owes her promotion to manager of her group to her level 3 Diploma and re-cognises that this allowed her to radically restructure a pre-school that had previously been run by two semi-trained staff, quasi-legally, as a private charity. 'The whole thing changed really with me going to college.' Arianne worked in tandem with two subsequent Diploma students and together they were able to oust the existing leaders through their insistence that the group must have a management committee to function as a charity. Here she reveals the importance of all aspects of a taught course in turning capability into functioning – theory, practice, formal and informal support systems blending together to facilitate change.

> I knew what had to happen. I knew what I had to do legally to make it work, um. I knew what it was that I had to put into practice from what I knew from being at college, from being here at work and from listening to all the other people at college – what they all did. So I knew that I could do it. And also, um, I knew that I could pick up the phone to somebody, either to yourself or to one of the other girls. I knew that somebody would be there.

Barbara was promoted to a post of responsibility as a result of qualifying to level 3, in her case to one of two deputy posts in a large village pre-school offering all-day care. The Diploma was a requirement of her employment and the job, which was 'very hard work sometimes', 'just seems to have opened up a wider career path'; one that may become even wider when Barbara completes her foundation degree. She is not yet ready to contemplate this possibility but admits that her eldest daughter is continually suggesting that she could earn more elsewhere.

These are the students who having qualified, moved up or moved on and turned their capabilities into new functionings. For the majority, changes are less dramatic but they are nevertheless identifiable.

Inching forward

Barbara was not unusual in seeing her decisions as a family concern. Qualifying only opened up new prospects if a student felt free to move on. Women returners continually considered the effect of change on partners and children. Note how Felicity worried about childcare arrangements during the summer when she anticipated her new advisory role:

> I'm hoping that this flexible hours thing will just work around them. I mean the summer holidays will be the testing time but that's the biggest holiday we've ever got to get through.

Frieda's options are limited by her children's needs too: 'They are still too young to be left in the school holidays for seven hours a day'. She pondered and planned ahead for over two years before swiftly moving on when a suitable job was advertised.

A mother would often make a move when she felt her children were old enough for her to work longer days. Bella, for example, made her first upward move when her daughter 'was going up to primary school' and she thought: 'I can do more ... now'. Conversely, for Irene the age of her children is a factor in her discontinuing a stressful job.

> I thought the age my children are and how much time it is taking up and it didn't seem right for me to be carrying on.

The interviews showed repeatedly that a job change, as an important influence on life-style, was not a decision made lightly or swiftly. Many students who do change jobs stay within the sector. Students appear to be fully aware of the capability set they occupy and demonstrate an opportunist attitude to suitable new jobs which is not dissimilar to the process whereby they initially entered childcare – because it was possible. In part this not-quite-settled atmosphere may derive from their awareness of the limitations in the workplace, discussed more fully in chapter 6.

Actually moving on, however, whether within or out of childcare was a slow and considered process and some students exhibited a surface flexibility alongside a hidden reluctance to risk making changes. Fiona described a long period of reflection before deciding to train as a nurse, and Ingrid is looking around for a TA job in a school but is prepared to wait a while before changing direction: 'I think it will depend on how things go with it in the next few years'. Imogen, a younger and childless student, also finds it difficult to move on quickly and cleanly, debating whether to apply for the post of unit co-ordinator in her nursery rather than go to university and whether to work part-time if she registers for a degree. Gina, who declares that she is happy for the time being, is nevertheless considering options – running yoga classes for babies or teaching either older or nursery age children. Even Diane, who had 'always given myself five years' at pre-school, found it difficult to leave. She described an early job interview as an embarrassment, 'because everything really came out about the way I was feeling and that really affirmed for me that it was then time to move on'.

This contradictory behaviour did suggest a possible connection between childcare work and a form of continuing 'maternal drive', as many of the students appeared to be tied to their own children and to those with whom they work, demonstrating a form of 'attachment' in Bowlby's (1969) sense of the term, together with a reduced sense of personal agency. But the difficulty in moving on could merely be inertia. When lives are carefully integrated to balance family, work, and education, any change has consequences for all the strands, favouring the maintenance of the *status quo* or gradual change: the most common pattern in these narratives. Indeed, the occupational typologies demonstrate the incidence of gradual change. Perhaps government policies which offered higher status and improved pay might induce more workers to stay in the sector once their own children become independent, and turn settlers and switchers into step-uppers.

Seeking better conditions in schools

For students actively seeking better terms and conditions after qualifying, working in a school as TA is a popular move. It leads to regular hours, a reduction in responsibilities and administrative tasks and in many instances a slightly higher rate of pay. Beryl managed to find a TA post even before the course finished. Holly talks of her daughter 'going to school for a half day' of starting as a parent helper 'in the school here' and how a TA post 'come up'. Deirdre was seeking shorter hours because when she was working nine-hour shifts in a day nursery: 'I never actually saw my children'. Aileen claims her TA job 'created a dramatic improvement in salary' compared to co-running an early years co-operative. Evelyn, however, appeared to be volunteering in the school as much as working (see chapter 5). Frances, who experimented with running an after-school club as a business for a year before seeking more regular hours as an administrator in a school, recognises the value of her change of job in salary terms: 'I definitely did need more money and I had to go out to work otherwise we wouldn't be living in this house'.

Decisions to stay in or move on from childcare after qualifying were neither lightly made, nor made for the reasons one might expect.

Focusing frustration

Comments about pay were common among the step-uppers and those who moved out of childcare, like Frances, but for the majority better pay was not a major consequence of attaining a vocational qualification. Unless a student changed jobs salaries were rarely mentioned. I questioned students in cohort 'J' to find out why this was so and found that many were paid the minimum wage and expected rises of between 5p and 20p per hour on qualifying – amounts they considered hardly significant, and further evidence that pay was not the key motivating factor for most staff. If students were being exploited financially it was not a major issue for them; other positional factors were more important.

For a few students becoming qualified *created* dissatisfaction. Their increased knowledge base raised their expectations and sense of self-worth. They wanted better treatment in the workplace and greater recognition at national level. Frieda stated this clearly.

> When you are taught how to do it ... you start to think 'hold on, I'm not being paid enough for this now ... I'm undervalued now because I know more'.

Where this dissatisfaction aligned with poor workplace conditions, the student did demonstrate agency and move on or out. Some stayed in childcare but became increasingly disillusioned. Frieda expresses this dissatisfaction most forcefully perhaps, becoming angry with both the general public and national government.

> Nobody actually outside the job really understands how much responsibility you hold – and how high the standards have to be ... there is still this kind of public notion that you just have a cosy little job down at the school and you are just a mum who's got a nice little job and aren't you lucky you get the holidays off ...

She wants conditions in the early years sector to have parity with teaching.

> It makes me really cross because I don't see how our successive governments can insist on raising, raising, raising standards but not actually taking on board any of the responsibility themselves for the people that they are asking to provide those standards.

Frieda is trapped in early years work by her own passion for it: 'I enjoy the challenges ... but the stress levels relative to the financial package are just ridiculous'.

Educational impacts
Residual learning

During the interviews, students were specifically asked to comment on the course content, as few did so without prompting. Even when asked directly, they only answered in general terms, referring to subject headings rather than syllabus detail. This made it difficult to assess the extent of their learning in terms of curriculum knowledge. About a third found planning very useful, a third mentioned child development. More specific comments were as diverse as the student group itself: a few enjoyed theorists, observational skills and play activities and some wanted more practical content.

The comments about missing subjects reflected individual specialisms. Irene mentioned teaching strategies, Alex would have liked more child protection training, and Danni more management tips. Several students wanted more information about special needs and behaviour management. Generally these comments reflected individualised interests that lie beyond a level-3 syllabus suggesting that the course did cover the necessary content quite thoroughly. A number of students in the later cohorts (G, H, I) found all the content equally useful whether they were experienced or novice practitioners, suggesting that students cannot immediately identify salient learning.

Some students, however, could recall details that demonstrated significant application of learning. Imogen comments on the 'little things' she found useful: lowering fans to children's height in hot weather, laying out pencils so that children naturally use a tripod grip, making individualised matching games based on their names. She tried out all these ideas in her group even though 'no one would listen to me at the nursery'. For Ingrid style was significant. She learned from real anecdotes: 'the experience you had ... from other playgroups or with your own children ... brought a lot of it into perspective for me'. Ingrid described her own changing perspectives, explaining that she could 'now look at the bigger picture' and seek out reasons. As her tutor, I value her comment that: 'You then taught us to sort of look *behind* the behaviour', as it reveals the presence of deeper learning.

Learning processes

Students with developed abilities tended to take them for granted and focused on deficits. This was true even for the graduates. Amy, for instance, studying alongside younger students on the play specialist course, became aware of the lack of presentation skills in the Diploma. Arianne and Frances, who are both given to self-reflection, described their own learning in terms of learning styles, demonstrating a knowledge of learning theory. Frances, Heena, Irene and Ilsa clearly preferred an active learning style, as they wanted more practical learning.

Students who were acquiring study skills tended to focus on the processes. Irma claimed that you 'just sit and listen, write everything down', Fiona talked about 'how to write essays' and Emily picked out prioritising time as the most important element for her. Heidi described studying as a set of procedures to follow:

> It's really hard doing all the reading when you had to find out all these quotes and that and finding the right bit and knowing what you mean and what they mean if you see what I mean.

Cindy also takes a stepped approach to learning, itemising each stage. 'The assignments were good, like they showed you how to do observations and stuff ... and you just knew how to understand, how to write them, and how to plan from them'. Her comments on her subsequent foundation degree training were very literal:

> It is quite heavy and you have got to read loads of books and make up references ... when you write your essays and stuff, if you use a quote from a book you have to make sure that you put that down and who it was by – by name.

To some extent all the comments on study skills have a 'know how' rather than a 'know that' feel but what is interesting is that it is the students who are formulating the steps to make sense of their learning, not the tutor. This suggests that linearity is an internalised process. It is perhaps disappointing that acknowledgements of residual learning are so limited but maybe this is inevitable in a retrospective study, or it might be a consequence of the broad focus of the interviews. It is possible that learning that has been truly assimilated is no longer readily isolated for recall but this does not mean that we should discount its existence or value. The gains are probably the changes in levels of learning style (Belenky *et al*, 1997/86), discussed in chapter 6, and the opening up of opportunities deriving from a confidence to undertake further study.

Further study

The Diploma served as an introduction to further study for a number of students. Amy enrolled on a hospital play specialist course, Barbara and Cindy have started a foundation degree and Heena is about to do so. Felicity has successfully completed a foundation degree already and Danni tried the course but for the time being at least has dropped out. Frieda, Holly and Bella mention a degree as a future possibility and Irene, Barbara and Gina may, in the future, enrol on teacher training courses. Emily completed a massage course but decided that a career working from home would be too lonely.

Some students have become lifelong learners. Holly has completed teaching assistant courses at levels 2 and (now) 3, a counselling course, sign language and sundry other short courses. She plans to take any school-based training course she is offered and is 'feathering' her nest 'to make it bigger and better'. Avril, who found education 'quite addictive', believes that as 'I'm in the habit now, I might as well go on, keep the ball rolling'. She has completed four significant qualifications and is considering topping these up to full degree level, but she doubts her ability because of negative feedback. Her concerns reveal that although a positive experience boosts confidence, this can easily be undermined.

Too much too soon

For a few students course attendance highlighted their lack of knowledge and experience. Emily, Gina and Irene all feared that they might have enrolled on the Diploma course too soon and felt that they would have benefited from more experience before undertaking it. Emily is measuring herself against a more educated colleague and this may account for her uncertainty. Gina was one of the students who sought a childcare course prior to finding a place-ment so her concerns are understandable, especially when faced with a room full of students of whom many were already working in a group. She was the only student directly to express the disempowerment associated with motherhood but I doubt that she would have been the only person to ex-perience this feeling.

> When you have been at home with children you do, you do somehow think the world has gone on without you to some extent.

It is likely that Irene's concerns are misplaced: it was possibly not the course but the taxing job of turning a struggling pre-school around, with little com-mittee support, that she had taken on prematurely.

Integrated lives

In addition to the thematic discussion in the previous chapter, it is important to look within the narratives and explore the significance of the combination of consequences for individual students. A holistic approach shows how individual lives develop and the role played by education in this process. The narratives demonstrated repeatedly that students juggle and balance their commitments, monitor their opportunities and marshal their strengths to achieve new functionings, and that those with children do this with a clear focus on, and acceptance of, their central role of mother. These are students who, in capability terms, are concerned with their current 'being' and 'doing', integrating aspects of their lives rather than trying to escape their domestic ties. They are flexible in their approach to life and accepting of the oppor-tunities that arise. Working within their capability sets, they seek outcomes that are personally achievable and, therefore, satisfactory. If we seek the bigger picture and look for connections across the life-course, we can pull to-gether threads that are dispersed throughout their discourses to demonstrate how individuals integrate their lives.

Celia who 'used to win poetry competitions' as a teenager before leaving school after a breakdown, found the Diploma useful in 'getting back into the mode of writing'. She would 'miss not working with children' but 'is throwing the towel in' because pre-school no longer meets her desire to be 'just caring for children' and the workplace is stressful. On asking why, I established that her 'marriage is falling apart' too, leading her to reassess her options. She actually says that 'I know from the Diploma I enjoyed putting pen to paper and creating sentences and words' and that she would like to 'explore the possibilities of anything creative – writing or art or anything and it would be child-based'. This is an attempt to integrate past and future and secure a change of lifestyle while she has financial security. Celia does not consider a return to her work in a riding school (after her breakdown) or her career as a young married woman, but decides to develop the interests latent at an earlier stage. A positive educational experience encourages Celia to repair a negative one.

Alex's mother, formerly a nurse, figures frequently in her narrative. Alex started a nursing course herself at 16 but only 'stuck' college for six months, extending her Saturday shop job to full-time and staying in the retail environment for eight years until her first child was born. She then helped in a pre-school and set up her own with friends, working weekends as a ward assistant at the hospital. The Diploma was essential to the childcare job and has since been useful in helping her deal with her son's problems at secondary school. She claims that both the 'knowledge into how the systems work' and the confidence deriving from success were important here: 'I am as good as the next one and I can go and check out whatever life throws at me'.

Becoming a single parent, she needed more money and runs a local newsagent's for a friend, starting at 6 or 7 am to be available for the children after school. This job is additionally attractive as the manager allows her children to come in for breakfast before school. Thus Alex has linked the Diploma knowledge to her children and made a return to retail employment. A further integration links the nursing and the 'people skills' aspects of childcare to the job. The shop is situated close to a drug dependency unit and Alex needs her confidence in dealing with vulnerable people to cope with this and to play an informal 'care in the community' role. Her retelling of individual addicts' life stories validates her claim that: 'I have actually had some good old conversations with some of them'. Thus the nursing and caring elements of her experience are also integrated into her current 'doing'.

We saw that Evelyn sought the confidence to overcome a mental breakdown stemming from an abusive marriage and that this was one of the outcomes of completing the Diploma. Having 'the confidence to go into school' includes a vocational element too. Before she had her children she worked as a carer, but when she studied she worked in pre-school. Thereafter, she moved into school to work with children with special needs, offering both educational support (for which her Diploma knowledge is essential) and personal care (which uses her caring skills). Thus she has integrated aspects of her life without sacrificing the chance to 'be at home with my children'.

Aileen's story centres on literacy and numeracy. Early in the interview she describes returning to college as a teenage mother to retake her maths, as 'I do feel maths and English are important'. When asked about the purposes of education, she mentions functional skills: 'as long as everybody can read and write and do basic sums we are halfway there ...'. After her pre-school folded, she chose a TA job where she used her Diploma knowledge but also did additional literacy training and has specialised in this area of support. Here we see a recurrent skills theme becoming a source of integration.

For Barbara, education has both a reparative and a prospective function. The Diploma made good the gaps in her general education and allowed her to pursue a career despite leaving school early to bring up a family. The foundation degree may enable her to progress later to teacher training. But the educational achievements play an important personal role in overcoming the 'stigma of teenage motherhood'. Despite a secure marriage and three healthy children she is looking forward to displaying her career and fitness at a school reunion when she turns 40. It matters that she will 'not be fat' and will 'have a career' whilst some of her friends are just having their first child. Here the connections are personal and have a linear trajectory, but nevertheless Barbara is integrating aspects of her life.

Frances achieved an integrated life, combining nurturing, organising and some creativity, after trying a series of careers. Early work as an au pair only linked to children. Later work in office administration excluded children completely but allowed her to adopt a supportive role towards her boss. We saw, in chapter 3, how her creative side finds an outlet in miniaturist pursuits but the Diploma showed her that product-led art was inappropriate for small children, making the pre-school an unsuitable focus for integration. We also saw that she set up an after-school club and tried to integrate childcare and administration by creating a set of policy documents, another short-lived attempt.

Frances now works as an arts co-ordinator in a secondary school and describes this as an 'ideal job' as it blends her love of the arts, her liking for children and her administrative skills which stem from her need for an ordered life. She believes the Diploma helped her to get the job, as she could demonstrate that she was ready to work and had a proven knowledge of children. More importantly, she considers that the Diploma improved her confidence, enabling her 'to go for the job'. As arts co-ordinator she can still adopt a child-centred approach but can work with small groups or individual older children so has no core need to concern herself with educational objectives or regulations and can befriend children as she sees fit. Thus she has found work that enables her to integrate several aspects of her life successfully.

For Ilsa integrated changes arise from the natural coincidence of making a career change from armed forces to childcare and having her own toddler. I see the changes we discuss as being part of her civilianisation. Ilsa does not acknowledge this interpretation, only that there was a 'huge process going on, a big huge process', but she does admit it was hard to find a job because she had 'been out of society for so many years'. In college she had to learn to fit into the group and to accept that not all learning can be 'bang, bang, bang'. In the pre-school setting she had to learn how to deal with colleagues and with children and this was not helped by false accusations of malpractice which were resolved only after an Ofsted investigation. At interview, however, she describes 'my *no mess* policy' and seems to have been able to find her own voice in dealing with children's discipline. The family aspect is fundamental to both home and work. Of the Diploma she says 'it made you think more about why ...' and the example she gives reveals just how important that was.

> And then my own child, it helped. Say before I wouldn't have realised that, say, he was tired and that was why he was being a bugger for two hours. I would have thought he was just being a bugger for two hours.

Holly had no choice but to change her life. Assaulted on duty, she could no longer work in the police force and sought a new career. Despite major physical consequences and agoraphobia, Holly shows a remarkable determination. She subsequently married and even though she had to wear leg braces and extensive body bandages to support her back and pelvis throughout the pregnancies, she had two children. She volunteered in pre-school and later primary alongside her children but acknowledges this supported her as much as them: it was easier to take them to school if she did not have to return alone. She likes to keep occupied as this controls her levels of anxiety: 'it kills off some of the ... if I do this, this will happen'. Continual retraining keeps her mind occupied but Holly also recognises that she is 'feathering my nest' in case she needs a better wage when her partner retires in five years time.

Holly is explicit about the ways in which her choices are integrated. She describes how, for a start, being a parent helper 'killed that coming home ... we'd come home together'. She compares the skills in observing children to those learned in interviewing witnesses: 'you are looking at everything ... I knew what I was doing right away', and knows she can 'transfer a lot of my skills what I'd had before'. Family is important too, as she recognises: 'if I learn all this I can transfer it to my children'. Thus past and present, personal and pre-school issues are all integrated in Holly's meticulous attack upon agora-phobia: 'Everything in my life was planned'.

If space allowed, I could demonstrate the integrated aspects of all the students' lives but instead, I offer some brief overviews. Amy's Diploma and earlier degree together led to success at an interview for a play specialist post. Diane uses the community and health and safety aspects of the Diploma with her geography degree when working for a countryside organisation. Irene and Gina know their graduate status and the Diploma will facilitate teacher training. Fiona's twins with special needs led to her crusade to help other such children, and a switch from childcare training to paediatric nursing. Frieda, so vociferous about levels of support for childcare workers, finds a job where the pre-school links to the reception class so she can continue the job she likes but with some state support. Imogen uses her A-levels and childcare experience to access a full-time psychology degree when the workplace turns out to be too stressful, choosing a course with significant child-development content. Felicity, a former bank employee, manages a successful pre-school and completes a foundation degree. When her children can cope independently, she takes a post as a business and enterprise officer in the childcare sector where she can effectively use both her financial acumen and her knowledge of children. Greta, after her early education amongst children with special needs in the 'dame' school, pursues a series of caring careers and possibly uses the Diploma course to come to terms with her own childlessness. Unlike other interviewees Greta is aware of her different status, talks about her nurturing side, and found the content on 'working with families the most useful' despite deciding not to remain in the field.

At the time of the interview, Heidi was utterly confused about what to do next. Work clearly gave shape to her life, and achieving the Diploma should have made it possible for her to continue in her chosen career. Integration of life and work was working negatively for her, temporarily, at least. However, Heidi demonstrated a sensitive and empathetic attitude towards the children and an ability to think holistically and independently. She makes one of the most important statements in the interviews, as she poignantly links her own learning to the children's needs:

If you tie it all in together, there is no reason why you should ever have a child ever crying.

This comment puts the child at the centre of the outcomes. But we have seen in this chapter that the consequences of studying reach far beyond the course aim to qualify mature women to work in childcare. The real world is complex and the students manage their learning to integrate all aspects of their lives. We have seen how their discussion of confidence ranges from the personal to the vocational and how it has both reparative aspects (students making good their earlier negative experiences) and prospective aspects (students feeling ready to take on new challenges), both minor and major.

The student narratives demonstrate transferability of learning. The students apply their knowledge to their own children and the children's schooling, and to their interactions within broader society, in addition to recognising that it makes sense of the job. The individual vignettes clearly show that integrating life is a compound process wherein capabilities already developed can be used alongside newer skills to support new functionings, ensuring firm foundations for future actions. This engenders stability in individual lives and enables the childcare students to live at a pace that matches their children's developing needs. By carefully considering and continually balancing all three aspects of their integrated lives, the mothers maintain a focus on day-to-day life that allows gradual change without perceptible disequilibrium. I believe they have found a way of living in a slowly shifting present, a paradoxical notion that is explored more fully in the next chapter.

8

Meeting women's needs:
heeding women's strengths

In essence, this book describes and discusses how a group of women satisfy some of their own needs without visibly disrupting historical traditions or challenging contemporary norms. In so doing they display their inherent strength. Their thinking is flexible and their actions pragmatic, revealing an ability to form both supportive networks and secure niches within which to live in harmony. Individually and collectively, these women are balancing the different facets of their lives by choosing to study childcare. They are integrating the personal, familial and vocational aspects and using education to facilitate the process. To achieve this balance they are choosing part-time motherhood, part-time education and part-time work in a sector often seen as inferior 'women's work' and they are making these choices positively. Contrary to the deficit models that equate part-time with negative status, integrated lives theory presents a positive model for contemporary living, one in which – with a little extra pay – women can enjoy the 'best of all worlds'.

Revisiting the strands

At the personal level the women are avoiding cognitive dissonance, as their need to care for their own children fits well with the traditional part-time pattern of childcare in the local community. But the pattern is increasingly threatened by the government agenda for all-day provision to allow other women to work full-time. Being a mother is a core facet of the students' identities and when they talk of 'missing out' on time with their children, their remarks carry strong emotional overtones which demonstrate a need for a gentle transition from parent to worker. The ease with which parents of pre-school children can drift into childcare work, and the way in which the majority enrol on the Diploma without accessing advice and guidance in college, confirms that the students are treading an established pathway. Perhaps they gain the confidence to study because they know of other women who have already done so successfully. Childcare staff have a collective capability set that supports the move from private to public sphere.

Families benefit from this pathway in many ways. First and foremost the children are cared for by their own mother outside school hours and this is a parent who strives to be available for her own children rather than one who has no other choice, no alternative external commitments in her life. In practical terms, many students stress the importance of being able to work convenient hours that fit with the traditional school day and term. Secondly, the children benefit from the parents' growing knowledge of child development and of educational practices; and also from their ability to use this knowledge within the family context and to interact with confidence with professionals on their children's behalf.

The workplace benefits too, as these women are enthusiastic about what they do, making a commitment to the setting and the children over and above what could be expected. We have seen that for most of them income is not the main motivator and they do not consider themselves to be exploited. Being paid something and moving on from voluntary status are important but low rates of pay are accepted as inevitable – provided the family can afford it.

Some students appear to work for altruistic motives, supporting the local community by caring for other people's children, but there may be additional hidden status benefits underpinning these actions. Either way, it is a major benefit to society that young children are being cared for by people who like them, who know about them, and who choose to work with them, rather than those who have no other job option. We have seen, too, how women claim to develop greater tolerance and better communication skills through working alongside people from different backgrounds and this too benefits the local community. Even those who leave childcare continue to use the skills they have acquired elsewhere. Be they teaching assistants in schools, carers in other fields, clerks in educational administration, they take with them an ability to work in partnership alongside other parents.

Education significantly helps to make such achievements possible but it also helps create satisfaction. The women can monitor their achievements, gaining a certificate that publicly acknowledges their success. For many of the students, childcare work is a natural extension of the 'mothering' role, but for others it is just a potential source of employment for someone striving to balance the needs of the family and the workplace and find the energy to undergo relevant training. An integrated life may be the only manageable option. Study time is marginal and confined to private times to avoid disrupting family life but this inheres luxury status too: education is precious, an indulgence not to be foregone. If it were not truly valued, students would not complete the course. That they are doing so despite the pressure from other greedy institutions implies that they take a longer view and recognise the benefits of qualifying.

At a practical level, study time is scarce and efforts must be streamlined, so students choose vocational courses even if they hold liberal views about education. Assessment criteria that were initially criticised are favoured retrospectively because of the ways they sectionalised assignments, creating manageable chunks for piecemeal completion and minimising the demand for engagement. Transmission of knowledge, too, is construed as an efficient way of learning 'what you need to know', and the tutor is seen as an agent for filtering this knowledge and tailoring it to meet individual needs. Thus the tutor may be drawn into playing an essential part in the balancing of family, work and education, and if the tutor fails to honour this (unstated) role, students may worry about lost time.

Reviewing the links

Ironically, in providing tailor-made provision, colleges are exacerbating the students' marginal status, excluding them from the mainstream educational experience. Mature women are *in* college but not *of* college. Studying is a marginalised pursuit – unlike part-time work because many students allow unpaid work-related tasks to drift into the domestic space. Some see this as evidence of their commitment, others as a reason to leave the field but, whatever the viewpoint, it would appear that their *almost* economic character grants these activities a legitimate status not given to studying. That partners comment on excessive hours and stressful working conditions suggests that such activities are visibly carried out and their intrusion into family life justified; so even low-paid work has a status above personal study. Many student narratives reveal the continuance of fuzzy life-work boundaries – this is allowed because the pay-off is flexible working practices rather than longer hours outside the home. In some families at least, this flexible working attracts the censure of partners. Their view of paid work is more conventional – but they have wives to take on the domestic chores and childcare arrangements. The voluntary nature of entry into childcare work and the lack of professional status within the workplace partly supports such overlaps.

Read without emotion, the overall story suggests a hangover of traditional Victorian values with the women's needs put last within the family, but this is only partly true. There is undoubtedly a sense of traditional structures con-tinuing within many families, with the children and partners occupying stronger positions than the women themselves but there is no sense of oppression. The students are openly subscribing to this pattern, taking control of the integration of family, workplace and educational practices and bending it to their own advantage. They enjoy this complex existence and want to engage with each sector. When the women come together they enjoy the social aspects of education, the element of being in the same boat. The day in college has a time-out quality, studying is a treat, albeit a stressful one: a day out, a chance to meet up with other women and think about matters *slightly* beyond the domestic sphere. Although it could also imply an element of female solidarity – women together escaping the confines of family expec-tations – there is no evidence for this in the narratives. If students complain about restrictions, the comments are individualised against specific partners, not part of a collective argument. It would be difficult to describe the limita-tions on the women's choices in terms of adaptive preference for they appear to be aware and accepting of, even colluding with, any restrictions.

The common pattern of juggling the needs of family, work and education is a choice the women freely make and that they do so in no way undermines counter arguments about professionalisation of the workforce, about the needs of the economy or the women's right to a more realistic wage. These women enjoy being mothers and, as Evelyn says, 'want the best of both worlds': being able to work *and* being available when the children are at home. In supporting the women's right to choose that they voice so clearly, I have no wish to relegate them to a life of impoverishment, to devalue the emotional skills associated with caring, or to undermine government plans to raise standards in childcare, but I do support the women's right to choose their own lives. This includes supporting decisions that appear, in part, to run counter to feminist views of equality between the sexes. This *is* an issue that is controversial and it requires an explicit consideration of the role of gender.

Considering gender

Any book that exclusively studies women risks accusations of gender-blind-ness so we need to look back at how gender is visible and has been addressed within the text. At an individual level gender is overtly captured in the student accounts, in the childhood narratives of family and schooling that sometimes reflect the discourse of male domination (Goldberg, 1993) but more often the narrative of caring (Noddings, 1984). In trivial but significant ways, gender manifests in behaviour patterns on the course. It can be seen in groupings and pairings, in a focus on domestic needs, in a high level of informality in the classroom. In the workplace, it appears in tales of student support but also in complaints of petty and volatile behaviour, in gossip and in hearsay.

At a deeper level, gender is present in the focus on childcare work, the articulation of family and domestic responsibility, the micro-level application of social capital theory, and the discussion of greedy institutions, and these are examined in chapter 4. There is some ambivalence in the educational component here, as it operates on caring principles but offers a more balanced knowledge-based curriculum. There is ambiguity too, in applauding the ability of many mature women to juggle education and other commitments successfully when, as Penny Burke (2002) claims, this disregards the exclusion of those who cannot so cope and the consequent need for governments to fund educational opportunities adequately.

Connectedness, a theme embedded in the analysis, is also essentially gendered. It infiltrates the book in many ways: the desire to link theory to practice, to bring personal anecdotes into the educational arena, to share ideas and experiences, to blur the boundaries between the public and the private; also the desire to bring the family into the workplace, the workplace into education, the educational into the family – the very reciprocal actions that underpin the integrated triangle and embed the women's lives within the broader community. In addition to being a site for choice, the triangle can be seen to describe how these particular women 'make the social world safe', avoiding aggression through human connectedness, creating a caring ethos rather than a life bounded by masculine rules (Gilligan, 1993/1982:43); a set of attitudes implicated, too, in Osgood's (2006a, 2006b) call for an alternative professionalisation based on caring and respect for emotions rather than the imposed processes she terms 'masculinisation'.

Emotional work, however, is beset with problems. Whilst I have refuted any suggestion that the women in the study cohort were schooled to conform to a specific 'vocational habitus' I accept the partial relevance of Colley's (2006: 25) argument that emotions are '*goods* that are generated by women', and for which they receive very little remuneration from profit-based nursery chains. In the context of her research, this is evidence of classed and gendered exploitation.

The students in my cohort, however, come from a range of backgrounds and most are working in the voluntary sector. The work settings have charitable status and any profit must be spent on improving the education of the children so the mature women in my study are not being directly exploited by business organisations. At a societal level, however, they are working for very little pay and there is an issue about whether this is acceptable. We have seen that the women often voiced altruistic motives for working in childcare and found the work rewarding, leading me to consider Price's earlier claim (2001; in Colley, 2006:25) that saw the 'deployment of emotion in caring work' as an individualised moral decision on behalf of the worker. However, arguments that domestic labour should be properly recognised and caring work appropriately recompensed still hold but in that case women may lose control of the private sphere. Women's realisation that this could happen might actually help uphold the gendered division of labour and the feminised nature of the caring professions.

This leads us to consider women's work choices more generally and to recognise that this is an area that is still contested. In *Gender Transformations* (1997) and an article in *New Political Economy* (1999) Sylvia Walby claims that the relegation of women to the private sphere is changing but accepts that there are considerable age-related differences in overall patterns, with older women more likely to work part-time than younger ones. She ascribes the part-time status of older women to structural patterns in society, believing that many remain segregated in low status, poorly paid, part-time jobs because earlier in life they were barred from the educational and work opportunities that might have enabled them to pursue satisfying, well-paid, full-time careers that would cover the cost of quality childcare. This view confines women's choices within a patriarchal framework which originated in 20th century trades union activity concerned to protect male jobs and salaries by claiming a 'household' wage.

Whilst this historical pattern undoubtedly has some truth, it undermines the notion of choice that so clearly emanates from the women themselves. Seeking an alternative explanation, I found support in sociologist Catherine Hakim's work (1991, 1995, 1996) leading to the development of Preference Theory (1998, 2004). Drawing on both global statistics and fine-graded analysis, she asserts that women are actively choosing part-time work, 'having different life goals from men' (1991:113). Categorising a fifth of women as career-oriented, an additional fifth as home-makers, Hakim (2004: 14) concludes that up to two thirds of women in any country are *adaptives* – women who choose to combine employment and family work. Hakim (1995: 436) provides evidence that this pattern is visible among older childless women too. She finds that women who show some degree of work commitment enjoy work for its own sake and value the intrinsic features of a job. Others, seeking additional family income, value convenient hours over good pay (1991:108). Hakim describes 'very high satisfaction with part-time jobs' (*ibid*:113) and relates this to choice, viewing women as 'self-determining actors' who 'still choose occupations and husbands which maintain traditional views of women's roles' (*ibid*:114). My own findings bear out these claims, although formulated quite independently of Hakim's work, thus giving the notion of choice further credibility.

Extending integrated lives theory

Within this study the women's lives have been analysed in a number of different ways. Their narratives have been considered holistically and as distinctive but interconnected strands relating to family, work and education. Life stories have been examined at the level of the individual but also collectively: in groups, through the two typologies, and as a whole, through the theorisation of the triple triangle. At all times, adhering to the philosophy underpinning the capability approach, generalisations have considered the needs and strengths of the individual in society. The work on capability indicators and chains in chapter 4 fully recognises the complexity of real lives and the impossibility of predicting outcomes from individual characteristics, even though we can find patterns within the data. In chapter 3, the attitudinal typologies demonstrate the importance of human agency, whilst the occupational set reveal that life is flexible and that some women progress through the occupational hierarchies over time, while others enter the profession at a certain level and choose to stay there.

However, the triple triangle has an explanatory capacity beyond the coverage in chapter 4. And its association with the broader and accepted theoretical framework of Sen's capability approach justifies further investigation of the role of integration in the women's lives. The credibility of integrated lives theory lies in its origins: the way the concept of a triple triangle emerged organically from my further immersion in the research data when it proved impossible to neatly separate educational from familial and vocational aspects of the narratives. The association with Sen's work derives from awareness that both the integrated lives triangle and the capability approach describe a focus on the present rather than on what *might be* in the future. Sen talks about 'being' and 'doing' and wants policy to focus on 'what life we lead and what we can or cannot do, can or cannot be' (1987:16). The women in this study reveal a similar concern with present everyday life rather than what might be possible in the future. When they are planning ahead they are acquiring 'potential' rather than rushing into a new functioning – a pattern that fits well with Sen's notion of the capability set.

Chapter 4 examined a range of theoretical perspectives and traced the reciprocal links that defined the original triangle of integrated lives, showing how this fitted with the notion of the capability set. Here, I want to extend this analysis and examine the role of the triple triangle in shaping the women's place within the broader society and its strength in mediating change. So far we have seen how the triangle supports stasis in the students' lives, creating a stable space in which to enjoy the present and attend to the needs of their children whilst developing and maintaining a degree of participation beyond the family boundary. However, despite the focus on the present, the students are closely monitoring their decisions and adjusting their lives to match the pace of their children's development, allowing an element of manageable change into their current life plans. The notion of stasis implies constant re-adjustment, change in a controlled way. It points to an ecological model that rebalances itself whenever movement occurs within the system. Even when findings run counter to social expectations, real world research must acknowledge that individual lives are played out in a social context and the concept of *transitional spaces* offers a framework within which to further consider the significance of localised changes captured in the data.

Transition and growth

Personal growth is a maturational process requiring time for development and, for these women, is apparently achieved in parallel to the growth of their children. Rapid advances, consequent upon the 'policy hysteria' (Stronach and MacLure, 1997) of the current century disturb but do not necessarily displace embedded processes and practices that follow a biological rhythm. For the students, the focus on the present is not a denial of change or progress, but rather an acceptance that this can be allowed to happen organically at a human pace.

Whilst intrinsically important, early years education is traditionally a transitional stage for children, bridging the gap between the home and school: the children's private and public spheres. Voluntary attendance at pre-schools or nurseries accustoms children to life outside the immediate family in a play-oriented and informal environment where social rules exist but are flexibly enforced (Schaffer, 1996). Although changes in educational policy challenge this pattern (see chapter 2), the current research findings suggest that early years settings serve a similar transitional function for many women. They offer a developmental space between caring in the home and working outside the family and, with education, support the change from instinctive carer to professional worker. As they do for the children, the childcare settings offer the women a safe space in which to gain experience, confidence, skills and, additionally, a reason for seeking an externally recognised qualification.

The Diploma course, too, affords students a secure experience of life beyond the local community, a chance to rehearse an involvement with the wider world. Students clearly needed peer support to meet such a new challenge. They talked at length about being in an adult group, being in the 'same boat' and coming with or newly making a close friend. The way they could recall minutiae like who sat where, who smoked during breaks, who travelled with whom and the ease with which their peers studied, demonstrated too the infrastructural importance of the class as a support mechanism.

However, we cannot ignore the possibility that women feel oppressed by their confinement in the domestic sphere. A discussion of the early years setting as a transitional *safe* space suggests that women enjoy the female role of part mother, part worker. Being a full-time housewife or mother may be less attractive for some of them: how else would the most common consequence of educational involvement be confidence? Confidence 'to do' is forward-looking but confidence 'to be' implies a deficit to correct and even when the causes are traced back to incidents in childhood and compulsory schooling in particular, just being at home as a wife and mother is clearly not a curative state. Some form of external support and recognition is also necessary and the Diploma course and part-time work clearly fulfil this function.

Living in a slowly shifting present

That students so often drifted from parent to volunteer to assistant, implies that positioning the pre-school and training course as transitional spaces is a credible idea and, in turn, contributes to an understanding of how stable family lives move imperceptibly forward in real time. We can challenge a simplistic interpretation of the role of parents in bringing up their children because we can view this as an intergenerational process, with children's natural rate of growth and development reciprocally affecting the pace of parental development.

Role adaptation occurs indiscernibly for many women but for some, those who entered childcare specifically to avoid separation from their own chil-dren (Arianne, for example), the process is slower as they need to withstand the inward pull of the maternal bond and look outwards into a new social setting. However, many women who choose to work *with* children in order to care for their own children doubly avoid cognitive dissonance so the psychological benefits can be considerable. They are able to 'be there' for their own children but also to adjust the pace of life to give the children time to explore and question and learn new things at a rate that allows assimilation.

Despite needing to balance multiple roles, the students are satisfied with their present lives. They focus on what matters now, content to enjoy the *status quo* rather than seeking to progress. But this can obscure their constantly changing state. The continual adjustment to meet the demands of family, work and education allows change to happen, but in a concerted way. To achieve a goal requires a gradual realignment of the entire triangle, the modification of each aspect in turn to accommodate a new equilibrium. The directional pulls of the three different aspects create inertia. The two opposing forces prevent a radical shift in any direction, and this slows down, even disguises, the presence of change. I use the phrase 'living in a slowly shifting present' to capture this paradox – a projection of an overtly stable present underpinned by constant but less perceptible change – for the interactions are complex, the daily advances too small to attract attention. But change is inevitable, if gradual. The students are qualifying, and many are increasing their involvement in the workplace. Those who are mothers are broadening their focus, embracing the schools, clubs and other activities their children frequent as they grow older. Life is changing organically at a pace that allows assimilation. By focusing on the triangle, the women resist the externalised rate of change imposed by government initiatives. There is a 'time-out' feel to the students' lives that is reflected in the occupational typology. The categories of sampler, stager, settler, switcher and step-upper explore the (im)permanent nature of childcare work in many lives and together capture the differing structural contexts in which transition can occur.

On the down side, perhaps it is the transitional nature of early years settings, together with the workforce's ambivalence towards change, that perpetuates the sector's continuing marginality. This particularly relates to the voluntary sector but we should remember that education only becomes compulsory after a child's fifth birthday, so all settings are in a sense voluntary.

Conceptualising instability

Despite representing stasis, the triple triangle offers an additional explanation of the mechanics of change; one that relates to the sudden decision to act after a long period of deliberation, even 'dis-ease' – a pattern often visible in the data. The triangle is a flexible ecological model but very stable in form. The different contexts are quite tightly interlocked and it takes serious or coincidental changes to cause a student to break out of this capability set and leave the sector entirely. Nevertheless, as in any natural system, changes in any one area require the entire system to readjust. Major financial changes, marital break-up, children leaving home, severely unpleasant working conditions – or possibly major policy initiatives from government – upset the status quo. When these occur singly they normatively create a directional shift rather than threatening the overall structure. When two coincide for an individual the situation is more serious and more significant changes may result. A triangle can withstand pressure on one of its points but multiple stress factors affecting additional points may destabilise it.

Although this is providential rather than intentional, my use of free association interviewing techniques frequently tested this hypothesis. When a significant change lacked adequate explanation, gentle probing often established a more likely additional or different reason. It is this second factor that usually precipitates a decision to act. For example, Irma was leaving childcare because of her frequent miscarriages – a family reason – but at first claimed she disliked aspects of the work. Celia revealed a second factor – marital problems – which coincided with stress in the workplace she had tolerated for ten years. Daisy ostensibly chose agency work because it suited her family commitments, but when prompted she admits to having had two negative appraisals in the workplace. Other students coped with one area of instability by making minor readjustments to their life decisions, simply realigning their choices.

We can surmise, that the triple triangle has some explanatory significance for childcare settings. Early years groups, particularly those in the voluntary sector, become vulnerable when staff are faced with multiple stress factors. One person's decision to leave the group when her triangle becomes destabilised can become a secondary stress factor for colleagues, causing them to leave too and further destabilise the group. In the voluntary sector in particular, early years settings depend upon unpaid management committees and poorly paid staff: people giving freely of their time. The settings' management structures are ill-designed to withstand crises in staff lives and over the years it has been apparent that groups are often very settled for long periods, even resistant to change, but then suddenly face a major upheaval, lose several staff and then reform themselves. Thus, looking beyond the family boundary, the integrated lives model also offers a partial explanation of change and stasis in the childcare sector, explaining how committee-run settings that are superficially stable are actually very vulnerable and can rapidly destabilise.

Living at the micro-level

In integrating their lives around family, education and the childcare sector, the students personally side-stepped conventional economic goals, whether or not they supported partners who pursued these ends. Rejecting the pursuit of affluence, and, in many cases, arguing against change and its manifestations as it entails more paperwork, longer hours and greater professionalisation, the students renounced instrumental values, placing people and their well-being at the centre of any discussion.

The research evidence suggests that dominant educational discourses relating to economic prosperity and professionalism generally fail to address the key concerns of the student body. Observed links between the macro- and micro-levels were often tenuous and tangential. This requires an explanation. Since the macro-level initiatives sought change and any change is stressful, stress avoidance is a possible reason. Or possibly the process of integrating lives engenders introspection, or is so intrinsically fulfilling that it leaves little energy for involvement with the outside world. The students certainly have very full lives, but the way that they are reaching out into the workplace and the community and their involvement in education make truly insular explanations unlikely.

Perhaps the problem lies with the nature of the changes. The student narratives revealed an underpinning interest in liberal values and in universal concepts, the bigger questions that relate to the wider world rather than its political manipulation. So the participants' disregard for the macro-level structures might stem from the instrumentalism of the initiatives rather than any parochialism on behalf of the students. Choice, time, change, stability, altruism, agency, independence and interdependence are themes that run continuously through the narratives and the subsequent analysis. At micro-level, the students are focused on the minutiae of existence, but in practice their concerns have a much wider reach, contesting any inference that their lives are introverted. These are women who care about society.

The study focuses at the micro-level and the students refer to overarching values. But they largely bypass the macro-level at which politicians and policy-makers strive to impose structure on collective lives. Change imposed at this level is largely seen as an irritant, an additional complication in already busy lives. It appears that the students are practising what the capability approach advocates: a focus on 'what we can or cannot do, can or cannot be' (Sen, 1987:16). This may include altruism, a characteristic Sen attributes to 'agency achievement' or it may be limited to 'well-being achievement' or personal satisfaction alone. Certainly, the women's decisions to temper personal development with the needs of their children and family seem to be an active choice, and in capability terms, this explains the sense of satisfaction that emanates from their narratives. Sen, however, demands a greater commitment from society. He sees agency as more than personal action and asserts that it must include the right to empowerment by the State, a 'social commitment' (1999:xii) to at least the removal of 'substantial unfreedoms'. If the students' stories are to have any influence on society they need to contribute to decision-making at the macro-level: at the very least to suggest ways to make policy objectives more palatable and facilitative for those who want to study.

Considering policy implications

The research findings support the provision of a wider range of policy options, and an acceptance that people are capable of making sensible decisions when given the freedom to choose for themselves. The typologies identify how diverse student groups need different forms of enticement. Yet, even though we know that people cannot be forced to learn, education policy continually steers learners in specific directions. Sectorisation, capping levels, specialised funding streams and restrictive criteria for eligibility are forms of 'unfreedom' and should, therefore, be challenged. So should the continuing divide between vocational and liberal education that discourages the development of the rounded individual who enjoys learning for its own sake as well as learning how to do things. The separation of skills from everyday learning appears to be an unpopular move and several students who were delighted about the skills they acquired said they would not have deliberately enrolled on a skills-focused course. If policy steers were relaxed and flexibility reinstated we might create a genuine learning society, one that recognises that skills can be developed incidentally – embedded – when students are enjoying what they are doing and doing what they want. Not all students are able to modify their learning environments to suit their own needs as the women in this research have done. If we could increase the number of co-realisable options available to students we could perhaps put the joy back into learning, for other students and their tutors too.

If choices were offered and were attractive, people might be persuaded to engage more fully with macro-level initiatives. In the past, successful adult educational provision was demand-led. The Mechanics Institutes, Workers' Educational Association and the University Extension Movement, to name but a few of the better-known, were all created to meet learners' needs. The success of the Diploma course may well arise from its original connections with a grass-roots childcare movement where a humanist, people-centred culture predominated. In contemporary society, governments increasingly seek feedback from service users but this is acquired through structured surveys which ask simplistic questions capable of statistical manipulation. In reality learner feedback, so obtained, is used judgementally to impose targets for improvement, whatever the level of student satisfaction. This puts pressure on colleges and lecturers to find a narrower, more instrumental focus, further restricting variety and choice for students.

Yet the picture we have of students integrating and stabilising their lives suggests that at a societal level the freedom to choose can bring about localised contentment, increased family bonding and strengthened communities, and contribute to core values in unplanned but effective ways. Chapter 4 considered these choices in relation to the social capital framework and we must recognise that in cleaving to the private sphere and leaving higher-level economic and political action to their partners, the women are reinforcing gendered divisions within society. However, this understanding should not underestimate the value to society of such micro-level endeavour, not least in ensuring that children are cared for by people who do so willingly. Neither should we disregard the importance to the women of the freedom to choose their own lives, nor forget that the majority of their partners accepted, even encouraged, these gendered patterns of behaviour.

The students were actively taking what they wanted from the course, choosing liberal, vocational or academic learning to meet their personal needs. This flexible uptake is important, particularly for mature women who come from very different starting points. Not all of the entrants to childcare who use the Diploma route have had more than a statutory education so flexibility in course delivery is essential if they are to make good the deficits in their knowledge before progressing to work with young children. The students all had to achieve at level 3 before contemplating further study and many liked to progress in stages. So it is important that governments continue to recognise the value of both foundation and bachelor degrees as qualifications in their own right as well as stages on the route to EYPS (cc, and see chapter 2). Some students will be lost along the EYPS pathway if the initial journey is seen as too arduous. Some will want to stop at an earlier level for personal, family or economic reasons or because they seek a different career. If students are acquiring transferable skills, we must accept that some will choose to use their learning differently. However, society still benefits from this transfer – although in unforeseen and probably immeasurable ways. Educational goals, too, may be achieved through less direct means: personal motivation can lead to public good.

Students were enrolling on early years training for personal and familial reasons and only coincidentally meeting government aims to raise standards and increase childcare provision. Given options, however, students appear to make suitable and sensible choices that serve their own ends and those of wider society. This suggests that governments could safely consider offering a range of possible choices and trusting people to plan their own lives, just as Sen proposes. Yet in England, the current move is towards limiting choice. Training is to be standardised through the adoption of a single Diploma for the Children and Young People's Workforce that has a strong vocational orientation. This is a narrowing of opportunity. It totally fails to recognise how unplanned social payback can be significant at the level of family and neighbourhood structures and how this can be lost through the relentless pursuit of over-defined instrumental goals for education. We have seen how the practice of women training to care for children in the voluntary sector strengthens social capital at local level. This is vital, as it is where children learn social behaviour. We have seen how education and pre-school settings serve as transitional spaces, enabling women to return to the workforce when their children become more independent, which is important in an ageing society. They do so by stealth, at minimal cost to the state, as they efficiently recycle the skills gained from living as well as from studying.

When mothers study childcare, this educates and empowers them as parents, directly benefiting their children by raising aspirations in the home, and indirectly encouraging elements of intergenerational learning. Training parents to work with children also provides schools with a steady stream of teaching assistants, trainee teachers, and parent governors who have realistic expectations and meet government aims for greater parental involvement. In addition, open-access courses for mature women partly meet the social justice agenda: the supportive ethos encourages the participation of women who have few or no qualifications, taking them out of the hard-to-reach category. A significant number of women who enrolled nationally on the childcare Diploma were achieving their first level 3 qualification; others were updating skills or moulding academic competence to a vocational purpose. For society, these are all significant strengths that could easily be swept away when policy addresses childcare reform without considering what could valuably be protected.

Within childcare provision, change needs to be carefully planned and flexibly applied. There is no reason why all settings should become full-time and good reason for local communities to manage and staff their own services. An element of voluntarism brings new people and new ideas continually into settings and this could itself promote positive change. When workers come from a range of backgrounds and when many have prior experience as service users, this potentially reduces the need for extensive governmental monitoring: parents know what matters to other parents. Instead, pre-schools are subject to continual monitoring and inspection and, faced with requirements for exhaustive Criminal Records Bureau (CRB) checks, many groups are excluding volunteers. This closes the informal pathway to employment for parents and turns early childhood settings into closed units which are set apart from their local communities. As a result, the social networks that ensure children's safety are curtailed and local communities are released from collective responsibility for the children who live there – surely a tale of social capital lost?

Within settings, too, policy requirements can be destructive, however unintentionally. We have seen that childcare staff found the planning and record keeping excessive and the continual implementation of minor changes frustrating, and that some experienced staff were seeking alternative work. The exponential change within the last decade has shaken up the sector and forced those within it to rethink their priorities and strategies. Some, the most frustrated, have chosen to leave the field and this may be a necessary process if the sector is to adapt and alter to meet contemporary expectations. Too much change, however, is counterproductive, putting at risk the essential human values that underpin the care of our youngest children. Social cohesion, at least at the micro-level, is vital to society and parental involvement within the voluntary childcare sector has long provided this essential social meshing.

To allow practices to embed and to obviate the need for continual updating of paperwork, a period of stability would now be beneficial; but, as I write, banners on the Department for Education (DfE) website stating that statutory guidance 'may not reflect Government policy' imply an unspoken *yet* that make this outcome unlikely. Nevertheless, childcare staff do need time to reflect and to review their beliefs, as indeed, do we.

In its contribution to such reflection, this book draws attention to certain significant issues. Although it is based on a small-scale study and tells the stories of just one group of mature women who trained to work in childcare, we should not underestimate the importance of the views they hold. It is clear that many of the stories they tell and the activities they engage in have relevance to society. Their decisions are bounded by familial, vocational and educational concerns and they balance demands and advantages in their search for integrated lives, demonstrating that part-time commitment should resist a deficit label. The women are freely choosing to put their children first, to work flexibly, to gain qualifications, and to play an active role in their local communities. They enjoy their lives and focus on their current opportunities rather than endlessly striving towards long-term goals. Future functionings are developed from current capabilities and, according to temperament, students may *accept* what arises naturally, *agonise* over decisions, progress through stages *accumulatively* or *assert* themselves to achieve change.

Women enter the childcare profession at different levels and some will *sample* the work and find they prefer to move on, whilst others will *settle* in childcare, maybe *switching* from a former career and seeking promotion, a *step-up* in childcare. Others, the *stagers*, approach childcare work as a temporary activity; something to do while the children are young, but often to do well while taking time out from more planned careers. Whatever their aspirations or their prior experiences, most of the women are childcare workers, parents and part-time students, and the ability to combine these roles to support the education of future generations of children is at once an overt need and a hidden strength deserving of support and recognition.

Concept catalogue (CC)

Adaptive preference (AP)
■ When people are convinced that they are choosing freely but are actually confining their aspirations to the choices that are possible for them, they are adapting their preferences. Some degree of adaptation is inevitable so this term is usually reserved for situations where the economic, physical or political environment seriously reduces choice. AP is a form of coping mechanism whereby people in reduced circumstances find contentment.

■ For a detailed but complex discussion *see* Jonathan Elster's chapter in Sen, A and Williams, B (1982) *Utilitarianism and Beyond.* Cambridge: Cambridge University Press.

Atrocity stories
■ Relates to a tendency within health care for patients to retell their encounters with medical professionals as if they had played an agentive rather than a passive role. Through exaggerated, often critical accounts, the patient retrospectively tries to redress the power imbalance of an unequal encounter. The stories are intended to justify the interviewee's actions or non-actions and restore self-esteem, also to seek interviewer approval. Thus they may occur in any situation where there is an unequal power structure and the 'weaker' person feels the need to save face by appearing 'in the right'.

■ This concept was first identified by Webb and Stimson (1976) and was tested and developed by Geoffrey Baruch in 1981 (*see* Moral tales: parent's stories of encounters with the health professions. *Sociology of Health and Illness* 3(3) p275-96). It is used more broadly as an analytical framework by David Silverman (2005) *Doing Qualitative Research* (2nd ed). London: Sage.

Bourdieu's capitals
■ French Marxist philosopher Pierre Bourdieu (1930-2002) made sense of the differing power bases within society in terms of different types of capital. Economic capital describes the visible power of wealth but less obviously cultural capital des-

151

cribes the attributes that enable the educated within society to claim superior status and power over others. Symbolic capital is status-related, referring to the prestige deriving from association – from position and connection or by award. Social capital (cc) refers to the advantages stemming from membership of a group.

- The capitals framework enables discussion of relative assets within society. For a concise introduction to capital theory see Bourdieu, P (1997/1986) The forms of capital. In A H Halsey, H Lauder, P Brown and A S Wells (eds) *Education: culture, economy, society*. Oxford: Oxford University Press.

Capability
- The potential to achieve. The things that an individual or, collectively, a group of people could feasibly choose to be, do or have.

Capability approach (CA)
- A theoretical framework developed over a number of years by economist Amartya Sen (sometimes with philosopher Martha Nussbaum) to facilitate policy-making that incorporates individual choice. Rather than specifying a theoretically optimum choice (cc utilitarianism) or ensuring basic equal rights (cc rights-based policy) the CA suggests that governments should offer a range of options so that people can make the choices that best suit their own needs. This is fairer than offering a single 'optimum' choice, as individuals and groups have different abilities to 'convert' what they can access (cc conversion). Thus, a free-parking space might benefit a person with a car but be of no use to a cyclist. Given a choice the cyclist might prefer a voucher to purchase a better bike, or, if a parent, the opportunity to buy a child's bicycle. Using the CA a government could offer a range of options and let people select for themselves.

- *See* Sen, A (1999) *Development as Freedom.* Oxford: Oxford University Press.

Capability set
- The combination of options available to an individual or group at any one time; described by Sen as representing the freedom to choose. Capabilities that are aligned are said to be in the same *vector*. If choices are co-realisable (not mutually exclusive) more than one may be possible.

Children Act 2004
- Implements the *Every Child Matters* (cc) programme whereby each local authority must establish Children's Trusts to prepare and monitor the multi-agency Children and Young People's Plan; nominate a Lead Member and Director of Children's Services; and establish a Local Safeguarding Children Board. At national level it established the post of Commissioner for Children as a spokesperson.

Childcare Act 2006

- Developed from the *Ten Year Strategy* published in 2004, it formalises local authorities' duties to improve the *Every Child Matters* (cc) outcomes for all children, secure sufficient childcare for working parents and provide better information services for parents. It reformed the early years regulations and inspection arrangements, made compulsory the Early Years Foundation Stage and the Ofsted Childcare Register and authorised the collection of data on young children.

Cognitive dissonance

- The discomfiting mental process of simultaneously holding two contradictory viewpoints. People are averse to this tension and seek ways to alter one view to align with the other, commonly through self-justification or false rationalisation.

- See Festinger, L (1957) *A Theory of Cognitive Dissonance.* Stanford: Stanford University Press.

Conversation analysis

- Provides formats for analysing the structures in talk to facilitate meaning and comparison. Speech is set out as a series of turns or 'utterances' and simple coding techniques capture changes in tone, pitch, speed or volume. This draws attention to the purposes of utterances. For instance, a comment like 'pleased to see you' would be classed as a demonstration of manners rather than as literally conveying pleasure. An examination of 'detritus' – ums, ers – reveals hesitation. One person 'cutting in' on another may reveal power inequalities. CA researchers treat talk as 'interaction' and confine their analysis to the speech itself but I have chosen to use it to capture meanings that were not directly verbalised.

- *See* Ten Have, P (1999) *Doing Conversation Analysis: a practical guide.* Thousand Oaks: Sage.

Conversion

- The process of turning a capability into a functioning, of making a particular option suit an individual's own purposes. For those with high levels of capability this may be achieved more readily than for those with lesser potential. The less advantaged may require a greater resource to equalise the opportunities from a particular action or perhaps a different approach altogether.

Dame School

- Privately run elementary schools catering for working-class girls, common in England in the 18th and 19th centuries. Usually a single, self-styled mistress set herself up in an annexe to her own home or to a community building and charged a small weekly fee to teach children obedience, manners and the basics of reading, writing and arithmetic; sewing too. In many schools the focus was on minding children, resources were poor and discipline could be harsh.

■ Greta's description reveals this to be an appropriate, if anachronistic, label for her 1960s private school that largely catered for children with special needs. She describes wooden desks with slates (no longer used) set in two hall-like buildings surrounded by tarmac, two elderly teachers and strict discipline involving sitting with a straight back and folded arms (but by 1960 mustard was no longer actually put on tongues). The curriculum abjured play and practical activity but included an annual 'sports day' with teams taking turns to run along a white line to catch an uncooked potato on a fork. Literacy was taught through Royal Readers and Victorian handwriting with 'incredibly great flourishes'.

Early Years Foundation Stage

■ Officially 'A structure of learning, development and care for children from birth to five years old' to be followed by all registered early years providers in the private, voluntary, independent and maintained sectors. Compulsory from September 2008.

Ecological framework

■ A term borrowed from nature describing the interdependence of the elements in a natural habitat. In the human sphere, such a framework implies a balanced structure where inputs and outputs mutually adjust, thus linking to systems theory. The phrase was coined by Urie Bronfenbrenner. Drawing on Kurt Lewin's work in social psychology, he classically represents influences on humans as a series of hierarchical circles radiating outwards from the micro- to the macro-level.

■ *See* Bronfenbrenner, U (1979) *The Ecology of Human Development.* Cambridge Ma: Harvard University Press.

Educare

■ A phrase blending education and care, popular among early years educators in the 1990s with the impetus to debate issues of quality and professionalism within the sector.

■ See the first edition of Anning, A and Edwards, A (1999) *Promoting Children's Learning from Birth to Five: developing the new early years professional.* Buckingham: Open University Press.

Emotional capital

■ Defined as 'The emotional resources passed on from mother to child through processes of parental involvement'.

■ *From* Reay, D (2000) A useful extension of Bourdieu's conceptual framework?: emotional capital as a way of understanding mothers' involvement in their children's education? *The Sociological Review* 48(4) p568-85.

Every Child Matters (ECM)

■ A government initiative with widespread impact, based on a 2003 Green Paper. It incorporates five main aims for children (to age19). To: Be healthy, Stay safe, Enjoy and achieve, Make a positive contribution, Achieve economic well-being. *Every Child Matters: change for children* (DES, 2004) set out a national framework to improve local services for children and young people, implemented through the 2004 Children Act.

Free association interviewing

■ A method adapted from psychotherapy. It seeks the *gestalt*, or bigger picture, by questioning how and why people make certain statements rather than accepting what they say as the complete truth. In its more general usage, the interviewer listens to oddities in the structures of the speech, finding connections in the juxtaposition of disparate ideas, denials in contradictions, uncertainty in hesitations. Through listening closely, the interviewer hears hidden dissonance and further questions the interviewee in order to clarify meaning. This process gives the interviewer a clear role in co-creating interviewee accounts and facilitates deeper analysis.

■ *See* Hollway, W and Jefferson, T (2000) *Doing Qualitative Research Differently: free association, narrative and the interview method.* London: Sage.

Functioning

■ The capability that an individual or group actually chooses to adopt from the range available. Thus a functioning is a capability that is activated, something that a person is actually doing.

Gender

■ Refers to the socially constructed roles attributed to men and women, either masculine or feminine, whereas sex is used for biological characteristics, male or female. In the late 1970s and 1980s, second wave feminists responded to criticism that simplistic categorisation ignores the differences among women: gender was deemed to have raced, aged and classed dimensions. Following Judith Butler (1990) some consider that gender is not only a learned behaviour but one that is performative.

■ *See* Richardson, D and Robinson, V (eds) (2008) *Gender and Women's Studies* (3rd ed). Basingstoke: Palgrave Macmillan for a readable overview.

Greedy institutions

■ Institutions that demand total commitment from their members making it difficult for them to engage with any other activity. The institutions do not force compliance but encourage loyalty and commitment by other means so participants subscribe to their own exploitation. In the public sphere (cc) legislation curbs excess demands, for instance in the workplace hours and activities are regulated. In the private sphere (cc) however, activity is only voluntarily restricted and individuals have to learn to say 'no' to protect themselves from exploitation.

■ In theory, it is possible to belong to only one such institution but in practice, people may manage to juggle several commitments if it is possible to conceal this process from those making the demands. Thus women may manage to meet the demands of work and family by secretly 'cheating' on each: ordering groceries online during working hours or reading business reports while the children get ready for bed. In this study education, too, requires complete attention and the competing demands of family, work and education create a tension that frames the women's lives creating a stable ecological framework (cc).

■ *See* Coser, L. (1974) *Greedy Institutions: patterns of undivided commitment.* New York: Free Press, which examines political systems, domestic organisation and religious collectives.

Habitus

■ Pierre Bourdieu's term for the mental framework within which individuals make sense of the world in which they live. This structures their thoughts and behaviours but is modified by new experiences so can be transformed over time. Distinctive groups share a similar habitus so this can be used as a descriptor at society level.

■ For an accessible introduction see Jenkins, J (1992) *Pierre Bourdieu.* London: Routledge.

Holistic analysis

■ The process of considering the whole picture rather than examining constituent elements. This may refer to a combinatory process whereby pieces of evidence are examined together but also commonly refers to a less structured practice of immersion in the data.

Human capital

■ Refers to the skills, competences and personal attributes that individuals contribute to the processes of production. Traced back to Adam Smith and other philosophers in the 18th C but popularised by Americans in the 1960s.

■ *See* Becker, G (1993/64) *Human Capital: a theoretical and empirical analysis, with special reference to education* (3rd ed). Chicago: University of Chicago Press.

Hygiene factors

■ Psychologist Frederick Herzberg, discovered that motivation at work focuses at two distinct levels. Hygiene factors are those we take for granted: the basic needs relating to working conditions, salary and security, that must be met to prevent dissatisfaction. In themselves, they do not encourage people to do better. Motivators, however, are less tangible, allowing the possibility of growth. For example, achievement and recognition, responsibility and advancement.

- *See* Herzberg, F (1959) *The Motivation to Work.* New York: John Wiley and Sons.

Individualisation

- Describes the atomisation of society in late modern times when some see personal autonomy to be more important than social cohesion. The phrase is associated with Ulrich Beck (author of *Risk Society*, 1992) and his wife Elisabeth Beck-Gernsheim who, in particular, considers the advantages for women of living for themselves rather than others. Because individualisation espouses equality of choice it can be confused with the capability approach but there are very clear differences between the two philosophies. The Becks' position is self-serving, defying social connections; whereas Sen's approach supports the improvement of individual lives within a social context.

- *See* Beck, U and Beck-Gernsheim, E (2002) *Individualization.* London: Sage.

Liberal education

- Refers to education for personal enrichment and focuses on acquiring knowledge and values to become a rounded individual and ethical citizen. Commonly voiced in the phrase 'education for its own sake' it can have elitist connotations in contemporary society as it stems from a period when only the leisured classes were educated.

- *See* Wallis, J (ed) (1996) *Liberal Adult Education: the end of an era?* Nottingham: University of Nottingham, Continuing Education Press.

Lifelong learning

- Refers to the process of learning throughout the life-course but mainly beyond the compulsory sector. In the 1970s UNESCO endorsed the phrase 'lifelong education', with implications that this should be publicly funded. Critical educators believe that the name change to 'learning' demonstrates a subtle shift of responsibility onto the learners themselves.

- *See* Field, J (2006) *Lifelong Learning and the New Educational Order* (2nd ed). Stoke on Trent: Trentham Books.

Managerialism

- The belief that generic management skills are applicable to a range of organisations despite any differences of purpose. This leads to the creation of a management team with little sector knowledge whose practices cut across those common to the profession. Often very systematised, with a focus on measuring performance and imposing standard procedures rather than more nuanced values. This practice undermines the professional identities of staff who hold qualifications and experience that are sector relevant.

■ *See* Holloway, J, Lewis, J and Mallory G (1995) *Performance Measurement and Evaluation*. London: Sage.

Narrative analysis

■ This takes a storied approach, considering people's accounts of themselves in their entirety rather than detecting individualised themes for cross-narrative comparison. A literature search will identify that a broad range of approaches fall under this label.

■ *See* Bryman, A and Burgess, R G (1994) *Analyzing Qualitative Data*. London: Routledge.

National Vocational Qualifications (NVQs)

■ Work-based awards requiring candidates to demonstrate their competence (ability to perform) against a range of sector-specific occupational standards graded from levels 1 to 5, senior management. Over the years, providers have tried different formats for assessment: work visits, portfolios, written reports, online paper-free recording; and different ways of introducing underpinning theoretical knowledge but the qualifications still tend to perpetuate existing practices rather than promote improvement so are subject to criticism in both the workplace and educational establishments.

■ *See* Wolf, A (2002) *Does Education Matter? Myths about education and economic growth*. London: Penguin.

Panoptic surveillance

■ Translates literally as 'all-seeing monitoring'. The panopticon element has physical origins in buildings: military schools and prisons planned to a circular design so that all inmates feel permanently overlooked whether or not the warders are present. The phrase derives its currency from Foucault, who uses it as a metaphor for contemporary societies where human activity is increasingly observed and monitored to ensure public compliance and mechanisms created to promote self-monitoring.

■ *See* Foucault, M (1977/75) *Discipline and Punish*. New York: Random House.

Patriarchy

■ A society where men hold dominant positions within both family and the larger community and the inferior status of women is seen to be a 'natural' and acceptable state of affairs. Feminist thinkers challenge this situation, often ascribing it to capitalist structures in society where the division of labour in the workplace requires females to play the role of unpaid carers in the domestic or private sphere (cc).

■ *See* Walby, S (1990) *Theorizing Patriarchy*. Oxford: Basil Blackwell.

Preference theory

- Divides women in modern society into three main groups: work-centred women (20% of the population) who frequently remain childless from choice; home-centred women (20%) who rarely choose to work (including stay-at-home mothers); and adaptive women (60%) who choose to work part-time (maybe combining paid work and child-rearing). This challenges economic and sociological theory that treats all labour as homogeneous.

- *See* Hakim, C (1998) Developing a sociology for the twenty-first century: preference theory. *British Journal of Sociology* 49(1) p137-43.

Private sphere

- A term commonly used by feminist thinkers to describe the domestic domain of the household where women are required to clean and care for the family without payment and thereby remain economically and politically invisible, perpetuating gendered divisions within society.

Professionalisation

- The process whereby an organisation or sector adopts and adheres to a set of standards and codes of practice that define good practice. This includes processes for regulation and monitoring, and in ideal situations these are autonomous; forms of self-regulation. In the early years sector, however, change has been externally imposed through *Every Child Matters* policies, especially the *Early Years Foundation Stage*, and overseen by the Children's Workforce Development Council (CWDC) and Ofsted. Within the profession there is a concern that the changes have taken control away from early years staff, overriding their need to develop professional identities as well as qualifications, and to determine a discourse of professionalism that recognises the value of care and nurturance.

- *See* Osgood, J (2006) Deconstructing professionalism in early childhood education: resisting the regulatory gaze. *Contemporary Issues in Early Childhood* 7(1) p5-14.

Public sphere

- The world of economic and political activity where men make and enforce decisions for society, able to participate freely because women provide unpaid domestic support within the home, perpetuating gendered divisions within society and angering feminist thinkers.

Radical education

- Radicals are those who get to the root of things and question the fundamental premises underpinning dominant beliefs. Thus, looking back through the history of education, the term is associated with reformers seeking to educate the working class, to raise their political awareness and instruct workers in literacy and numeracy. Hence there are parallels with basic skills teaching in contemporary society. However, the term also refers to alternative educational systems.

■ *See* Lovett, T (ed) (1988) *Radical Approaches to Adult Education: a reader.* London: Routledge.

Rights-based policy

■ This takes various forms. For Libertarians, the individual's rights to life, liberty and property are fundamental, not politically derived; for Contractualists, rights are determined by a social contract to which governments must adhere. Both philosophies focus at the level of the individual in society and treat everyone the same regardless of need, thereby disallowing choice and positive discrimination.

Schemas

■ Early patterns of behaviour, seen as repetitive actions in babies. These form the basis of all learning, gradually becoming more complex and co-ordinated. In toddlers these become more abstract, supporting children's patterns of thought, and evident in speech and mark-making as well as action. Examples include 'back and forth' and rotation.

■ *See* Athey, C (1990) *Extending Thought in Young Children: a parent-teacher partnership.* London: Paul Chapman (academic coverage); Nutbrown, C (2006) *Threads of Thinking: young children learning and the role of early education* (3rd ed). London: Sage (practice orientated).

Social capital

■ Describes the everyday networks, ties and customs that unite a community; recognising that the support the individual gains from such connections is an asset, despite having no direct monetary value. For instance, a person who has lived in a community for a long time and knows lots of people may be able to request many favours on encountering a period of hardship, so has high levels of social capital.

■ The phrase has origins in many early philosophies but was named by Bourdieu and taken up by, for example, Coleman, Putnam, and Fukuyama. Social capital components include: networks; clusters of norms, values and expectancies that the group members share; and sanctions to protect the networks and norms of behaviour. This sounds formidable but in practice, sanctions can be as little as a raised eyebrow, a public snubbing or exhortation to do something.

■ *See* Halpern, D (2005) *Social Capital.* Cambridge: Polity Press.

Spiral curriculum

■ Bruner's notion that a curriculum should repeatedly visit ideas to ensure student understanding, building in more complex interpretations as students grasp the ideas that are being taught. An important facet of his belief that concepts can be simplified and taught at an early stage, contradicting Piaget's notion of readiness to learn.

■ *See* Bruner, J (1960) *The Process of Education*. Cambridge, Ma: Harvard University Press.

Therapy culture

■ Coined by Frank Furedi, this concept refers to the practice of imposing conformity by managing people's emotion in the guise of 'emotional enlightenment'. Thus it becomes a powerful tool for social control, reducing the individual's sense of agency. The concept is applied to education by Kathryn Ecclestone and Dennis Hayes, who trace trends across all sectors that encourage teachers to move from academic instruction to therapeutic intervention. They see this process as 'profoundly anti-educational' because it undermines the knowledge purposes of education and 'dangerous' because it 'opens up people's emotions to assessment by the state' encouraging dependence (pxiii).

■ *See* Ecclestone, K and Hayes, D (2009) *The Dangerous Rise of Therapeutic Education*. Abingdon: Routledge.

Transition

■ In early years education, this term is often associated with transfer between establishments: home to nursery, nursery to primary class, primary to secondary school. However, in its broader meaning it refers to the process of change and this can be mental as well as physical and can take place over a considerable period of time. Thus when I refer to the pre-school and the Diploma course as transitional spaces, I mean that they offer an opportunity for change and adjustment before an individual takes on new attitudes or opportunities.

Tripartite division – tripartism

■ The Education Act 1944 made provision for a tripartite division of education into grammar, secondary technical and secondary modern schools but this was never fully implemented. This specialisation was earlier supported by the Victorian Royal Commissions and its origins have been traced back to Plato's division of the populace into three separate classes – guardians, auxiliaries and workers. Despite the social justice agenda this debate is still current, for example, in recent disagreements about the format for level 3 secondary diplomas.

■ For a discussion of trackers (seeking separate paths), frameworkers (supporting combination of existing paths) and unifiers (wanting a single, overarching structure), *see* Hyland, T and Merrill, B (2003) *The Changing Face of Education.* London: RoutledgeFalmer.

Utilitarianism

■ A moral philosophy, taken up in the 19th century, deriving from the work of Jeremy Bentham and later John Stuart Mill. It sees the goal of society to be the pursuit of happiness (later termed welfare), as this is the visible expression of 'desire' and therefore the only means of assessing what people want. On becoming the basis for government policy it was assumed that the utility, or satisfaction, a person would derive from a particular option could be measured and that these individual values could be added together to decide allocations of goods in society. People were assumed to be rational beings who would choose the options deemed to maximise satisfaction and thus, such policy would achieve, in Bentham's words, 'the greatest happiness of the greatest number'.

Vocational education

■ Education intended to prepare people for work, often termed 'training' and usually focused on a specific occupation or trade, as it focuses on 'how to do' tasks (or procedural knowledge) and not necessarily on underlying theoretical reasoning, although increasingly that absence is challenged at higher levels of study. In the UK, vocational education is seen to be in ascendance, following Geoffrey Callaghan's *Great Debate* speech at Ruskin College in 1976.

■ [Available at http://educationengland.org.uk/documents/speeches/1976ruskin.html, accessed 25 January 2011].

Vocational habitus

■ An adaptation of Bourdieu's original concept to describe 'the combination of idealised and realised dispositions to which students must orientate themselves in order to become 'the right person for the job'.' This must 'also include aspects of sensibility – of feeling and emotion – as well as the practical sense of what it takes to do a particular kind of work'.

■ *From* Colley, H (2006) Learning to labour with feeling: class, gender and emotion in childcare education and training. *Contemporary Issues in Early Childhood* 7(1) p25.

Women's ways of knowing

■ Concerned that William Perry's classic study of intellectual development in American college students allowed overgeneralisation from the male perspective, a group of American academics investigated the female position; creating a five-fold classification.

■ Using their original words, the categories are:

Silence: 'a position in which women experience themselves as mindless and voiceless and subject to the whims of external authority'.

Received Knowledge: 'a perspective from which women conceive of themselves as capable of receiving, even reproducing, knowledge from the all-knowing external authorities but not capable of creating knowledge on their own'.

Subjective Knowledge: 'a perspective from which truth and knowledge are conceived of as personal, private, and subjectively known or intuited'.

Procedural Knowledge: 'a position in which women are invested in learning and applying objective procedures for obtaining and communicating knowledge'.

Constructed Knowledge: 'a position in which women view all knowledge as contextual, experience themselves as creators of knowledge, and value both subjective and objective strategies for knowing'.

- *See* Belenky, M F, Clinchy, B M, Goldberger, N R, and Tarule, J M (1997/86) *Women's Ways of Knowing.* New York: Basic Books.

- *See also* Perry, W G (1970) *Forms of Intellectual and Ethical Development in the College Years.* New York: Holt, Rinehart and Winston.

Appendix: Typology attribution

Aileen **Settler** could become a *stager* if she does move on as she claims
Accumulater at lower level, but with some characteristics of *accepter*

Alex **Stager**, *sampled* many part-time jobs but only childcare when children young
Accepter, analyses like an *agoniser* but does not waste energy on the impossible

Amy **Step-upper** to play specialist
Accepter needs 'a little push'

Arianne **Settler** after varied retail/office work
Asserter 'I used to keep the class quiet' for school teacher

Avril **Step-upper** and **switcher** from business studies
Accumulater 'in the study mode so to speak'

Barbara **Settler** could become a *step-upper*
Accumulater 'I've got long term goals'

Bella **Step-upper** to nursery head
Asserter 'following what I think is right'

Beryl **Settler** or **switcher**? former arts graduate, could become a *step-upper*
Accepter 'see how it goes and see where it leads really'

Bethany **Switcher** from civil service
Accepter 'can't really see the benefits in leaving here ... finding something else'

Celia **Switcher** from veterinary nursing, could be a *stager* if moves on after 10 years
Agoniser 'I didn't fit in at all with the other girls'

Cindy **Settler** not quite a *step-upper* but approaching this as day centre manager
Agoniser with elements of *accumulater*

Daisy   **Switcher** enforced after head injury
                   Agoniser 'stuck for words'

Danni   **Switcher** could become a *stager* or *step-upper* if an opportunity arises
                   Accepter 'I'll give it a go'

Deirdre   **Switcher** chef originally
                   Asserter at times. 'Come on, I have to go shortly ... or I can always make a face'

Diane   **Stager** states this from outset, a *step-upper* in a sense but not in childcare
                   Accumulater with *accepter* tendencies

Emily   **Switcher** from retail
                   Accepter 'at the time, I went with the flow'

Evelyn   **Switcher** from social care
                   Agoniser 'I'm wondering if...'

Faye   **Stager** could be a *settler* if business does not do well
                   Accepter 'and then I kind of fell into it really...'

Felicity   **Step-upper** but was a *switcher* from commerce at sampling stage
                   Accepter 'let's apply for it and see what happens'

Fiona   **Step-upper** into paediatric nursing
                   Asserter 'if they would just point me in the right direction'

Frances   **Stager** now in administrative support role but still in education
                   Agoniser 'I do analyse myself ever such a lot'

Frieda   **Switcher** from insurance
                   Agoniser 'I would be lying in bed worrying about it anyway'

Gina   **Switcher** could become a *stager* if pay is pegged, or a *step-upper* into teaching
                   Accepter 'I just sort of moved into her position'

Greta   **Sampler** tries many different jobs
                   Agoniser with flashes of *asserter*, but *accepter* when seeking jobs

Hansa   **Sampler** resting postnatally
                   Accepter 'yes, I really had to work ... 40 hours a week'

Heena   **Switcher** from ICT, could later become a *step-upper*
                   Agoniser 'I'm quite an insecure person in things that I do'

Heidi   **Settler** after three attempts to qualify but currently resting
                   Agoniser 'And now I don't know which way to turn'

Holly   **Switcher** from police, could become a *step-upper* in teaching or EY setting
Accumulater some *asserter* tendencies in overcoming medical problems

Ilsa   **Switcher** from armed forces, may well become a *step-upper* later in teaching
Asserter but *agoniser* tendencies developing as life experiences impact

Imogen   **Sampler** may return as graduate *step-upper*
Agoniser 'I don't know, she might be a waste of space...'

Ingrid   **Switcher** but could become a *stager* if no promotion
Agoniser 'there is a need to analyse sometimes and a need to understand...'

Irene   **Switcher** could be *step-upper* if does teaching qualification
Accepter 'It might change again – probably not – but who knows'

Irma   **Stager** with elements of **sampler** as entry to childcare was reactive
Accepter but only to a certain level 'hmmm – can't see why not...'

References

Anning, A and Edwards, A (1999) *Promoting Children's Learning from Birth to Five: developing the new early years professional.* Buckingham: Open University Press

Arnot, M, David, M and Weiner, G (1999) *Closing the Gender Gap: postwar education and social change.* Cambridge: Polity Press

Athey, C (1990) *Extending Thought in Young Children: a parent-teacher partnership.* London: Paul Chapman Publishing

Audit Commission (1996) *Counting to Five: education of children under five.* London: HMSO

Ball, C (1994) *Start Right: the importance of early learning.* London: Royal Society for the Encouragement of Arts Manufacturers and Commerce

Baron, S, Field, J and Schuller, T (eds) (2000) *Social Capital: critical perspectives.* Oxford: Oxford University Press

Baruch, G (1981) Moral tales: parents' stories of encounters with the health professions. *Sociology of Health and Illness* 3(3) p275-96

Beck, U (1992) *Risk Society: towards a new modernity.* London: Sage

Beck, U and Beck-Gernsheim, E (2002) *Individualization.* London: Sage

Beck-Gernsheim, E (2002) *Re-inventing the Family: in search of new lifestyles.* Cambridge: Polity Press

Becker, G (1993/64) *Human Capital: a theoretical and empirical analysis, with special reference to education* (3rd ed). Chicago: University of Chicago Press

Belenky, M F, Clinchy, B M, Goldberger, N R and Tarule, J M (1997/86) *Women's Ways of Knowing: the development of self, voice, and mind.* New York: Basic Books

Bernstein, B (2003/1975) *Class, Codes and Control (3): towards a theory of educational transmission.* London: Routledge

Biesta, G and Tedder, M (2007) Agency and learning in the lifecourse: towards an ecological perspective. *Studies in the Education of Adults* 39(2) p132-49

Bourdieu, P (1997/1986) The forms of capital. In A H Halsey, H Lauder, P Brown and A S Wells (eds) *Education: culture, economy, society.* Oxford: Oxford University Press

Bowlby, J (1951) *Maternal Care and Mental Health, report to the World Health Organization.* New York: Shocken Books

Bowlby, J (1969) *Attachment and Loss: attachment.* New York: Basic Books

Brannen, J and Moss, P (1991) *Managing Mothers: dual earner households after maternity leave.* London: Unwin Hyman

Brehony, K (2000) English revisionist Froebelians and the schooling of the urban poor. In M Hilton and P Hirsch *Practical Visionaries: women, education and social progress 1790-1930.* Harlow: Pearson Education

Broadfoot, P (1999) Assessment and the emergence of modern society. In B Moon and P Murphy (eds) *Curriculum in Context*. London: Paul Chapman Publishing in association with the Open University

Bronfenbrenner, U (1979) *The Ecology of Human Development*. Cambridge Ma: Harvard University Press

Brostermann, N (1997) *Inventing Kindergarten*. New York: Harry N Abrams

Brown, S and Cleave, S (1994) *Four Year Olds in School: quality matters* (2nd ed). Slough: National Foundation for Education Research

Bruner, J (1960) *The Process of Education*. Cambridge, Ma: Harvard University Press

Bryant, M (1985) Reflections on the nature of the education of women and girls. In J Purvis (ed) *The Education of Girls and Women, Proceedings of the History of Education Society of Great Britain*. London: The History of Education Society

Bryman, A and Burgess, R G (1994) *Analyzing Qualitative Data*. London: Routledge

Burke, P J (2002) *Accessing Education: effectively widening participation*. Stoke on Trent: Trentham Books

CACE (Central Advisory Council for Education) (1967) *Children and Their Primary Schools (Plowden report)*. London: HMSO

Callaghan, J (1976) Towards a National Debate. Speech given at Ruskin College, Oxford on 18 October 1976 [Available at http://educationengland.org.uk/documents/speeches/1976ruskin.html, accessed 25 January 2011].

Cameron, C, Moss, P and Owen, C (1999) *Men in the Nursery: gender and caring work*. London: Paul Chapman Publishing

Cameron, C, Owen, C and Moss, P (2001) *Entry, Retention and Loss: a study of childcare students and workers*, research report no 275. Nottingham: Department for Education and Skills

Clarke, J (2002) Deconstructing Domestication: women's experience and the goals of critical pedagogy. In R Harrison, F Reeve, A Hanson and J Clarke (eds) *Supporting Lifelong Learning (1): perspectives on learning*. London: RoutledgeFalmer in association with the Open University

Cleave, S and Brown, S (c1989) *Four Year Olds in School: meeting their needs*. Slough: National Foundation for Education Research

Coats, M (1994) *Women's Education*. Buckingham: SRHE and the Open University Press

Coleman, J (1988) Social capital in the creation of human capital. *American Journal of Sociology 94, Supplement* S95-120

Colley, H (2006) Learning to labour with feeling: class, gender and emotion in childcare education and training. *Contemporary Issues in Early Childhood* 7(1) p15-29

Colley, H, James, D, Tedder, M, and Diment, K (2003) Learning as becoming in vocational education and training: class, gender and the role of vocational habitus. *Journal of Vocational Education and Training* 55(4) p471-96

Coser, L (1974) *Greedy Institutions: patterns of undivided commitment*. New York: Free Press [accessed online @ www.questia.com]

Cunningham, P (2000) The Montessori phenomenon: gender and internationalism in early twentieth-century innovation. In M Hilton and P Hirsch *Practical Visionaries: women, education and social progress 1790-1930*. Harlow: Pearson Education

David, M E (1980) *The State, the Family and Education*. London: Routledge and Kegan Paul

David, M E (1993) *Parents, Gender and Education Reform*. Cambridge: Polity Press

David, T (1990) *Under Five – under-educated?* Milton Keynes: Open University Press

DCSF (Department for Children, Schools and Families) (2007) *The Children's Plan: building bright futures – summary*. London: DCSF

DES (Department for Education and Science) (1972) *Education: a framework for expansion*, cmnd 5174. London: HMSO

DES (Department for Education and Science) (1985) Better Schools. London: HMSO

DES (Department for Education and Science) (1990) *Starting with Quality: report of the committee of inquiry into the educational experiences offered to three- and four-year-olds (the Rumbold report)*. London: HMSO

DfEE (Department for Education and Employment) (1998a) *Meeting the Childcare Challenge*. Sudbury: DfEE Publications

DfEE (Department for Education and Employment) (1998b) *The Learning Age: a renaissance for a new Britain*, cmnd 3790. London: The Stationery Office

DfEE (Department for Education and Employment) (2001) *The National Standards for Under Eights Day Care and Childminding: full day care*. London: DfEE

DfES (Department for Education and Skills) (2003) *Every Child Matters* (Green Paper). London: HMSO

DfES (Department for Education and Skills) (2007) *The Early Years Foundation Stage: setting the standards for learning, development and care for children from birth to five*. Nottingham: DfES

Ecclestone, K and Hayes, D (2009) *The Dangerous Rise of Therapeutic Education*. Abingdon: Routledge

Edwards, R (1993) *Mature Women Students: separating or connecting family and education*. London: Taylor and Francis

Edwards, R (2004) Present and absent in troubling ways: families and social capital debates. *The Sociological Review* 52(1) pp1-21

Elster, J (1982) Sour grapes – utilitarianism and the genesis of wants. In A Sen and B Williams (eds) *Utilitarianism and Beyond*. Cambridge: Cambridge University Press, and Paris: Editions de la Maison des Sciences de l'Homme

Festinger, L (1957) *A Theory of Cognitive Dissonance*. Stanford: Stanford University Press

Field, J (2006) *Lifelong Learning and the New Educational Order* (2nd ed). Stoke on Trent: Trentham Books

Foucault, M (1977) *Discipline and Punish*. New York: Random House

Furedi, F (2004) *Therapy Culture: creating vulnerability in an uncertain age*. London: Routledge

Gilligan, C (1993/1982) *In a Different Voice*. Cambridge Ma: Harvard University Press

Goldberg, S (1993) *Why Men Rule: a theory of male dominance*. Chicago: Open Court

Hakim, C (1991) Grateful slaves and self-made women: fact and fantasy in women's work orientations. *European Sociological Review* 7(2) p101-21

Hakim, C (1995) Five feminist myths about women's employment. *The British Journal of Sociology* 46(3) p429-55

Hakim, C (1996) *Key Issues in Women's Work: female heterogeneity and the polarisation of women's employment*. London: The Athlone Press

Hakim, C (1998) Developing a sociology for the twenty-first century: preference theory. *The British Journal of Sociology* 49(1) p137-43

Hakim, C (2004) *Key Issues in Women's Work: female diversity and the polarisation of women's employment*. London: Glasshouse Press

Halpern, D (2005) Social Capital. Cambridge: Polity Press

Hart, M (1992) *Working and Educating for Life: feminist international perspectives on adult education.* London: Routledge

Herzberg, F (1959) *The Motivation to Work.* New York: John Wiley and Sons

Hevey, D and Curtis, A (1996) Training to work in the early years. In G Pugh (ed) *Contemporary Issues in the Early Years: working collaboratively for children* (2nd ed). London: Paul Chapman Publishing

HM Treasury (2004) *Choice for Parents, the best start for children: ten year strategy for childcare.* Nottingham: DfES

HMSO (1986) *Achievement in Primary Schools, report of the Education, Arts and Science Committee* (1). London: The Stationery Office

Hodge, M (2000) *Matter of Fact.* BBC 1, 3 February 2000

Holloway, J, Lewis, J and Mallory G (1995) *Performance Measurement and Evaluation.* London: Sage in association with the Open University

Hollway, W and Jefferson, T (2000) *Doing Qualitative Research Differently: free association, narrative and the interview method.* London: Sage

Hyland, T and Merrill, B (2003) *The Changing Face of Education.* London: RoutledgeFalmer

Jenkins, J (1992) *Pierre Bourdieu.* London: Routledge

Lea, J, Hayes, D, Armitage, A, Lomas, L, and Markless, S (2003) *Working in Post-Compulsory Education.* Maidenhead: Open University Press

Lovett, T (ed) (1988) *Radical Approaches to Adult Education: a reader.* London: Routledge

McCail, G (c1986) *The 4 Year Old in the Classroom: an analysis of the responses of infant and nursery teachers to a BAECE inquiry.* London: British Association for Early Childhood Education

McGivney, V (1993) *Women, Education and Training: barriers to access, informal starting points and progression routes.* Leicester: NIACE

McGivney, V (2005) Are adult educators obsessed with developing self-esteem? [A debate with Kathryn Ecclestone] *Adult Learning* 16(5) January p8-13

Merrill, B (1999) *Gender, Change and Identity: mature women students in universities.* Aldershot: Ashgate

National Commission on Education (1993) *Learning to Succeed.* London: Heinemann

NFER (1987) *Four Year Olds in School: policy and practice.* Slough: National Foundation for Education Research

Nias, J (1989) *Primary Teachers Talking: a study of teaching as work.* London: Routledge

Nias, J (1991) Primary Teachers Talking: a reflexive account of longitudinal research. In G Walford (ed) *Doing Educational Research.* London: Routledge

Noddings, N (1984) *Caring: a feminine approach to ethics and moral education.* Berkeley: University of California Press

Nussbaum, M (2000) *Women and Human Development: the capabilities approach.* Cambridge: Cambridge University Press

Nussbaum, M and Glover, J (eds) (1995) *Women, Culture, and Development: a study of human capabilities.* Oxford: Oxford University Press

Nussbaum, M and Sen, A (eds) (1993) *The Quality of Life.* Oxford: Oxford University Press

Nutbrown, C (2006) *Threads of Thinking: young children learning and the role of early education* (3rd ed). London: Sage

Osgood, J (2006a) Deconstructing professionalism in early childhood education: resisting the regulatory gaze. *Contemporary Issues in Early Childhood* 7(1) p5-14

Osgood, J (2006b) Professionalism and performativity: the feminist challenge facing early years practitioners. *Early Years* 26(2) p187-99

Parr, J (2000) *Identity and Education: the links for mature women students*. Aldershot: Ashgate

Pascall, G and Cox, R (1993) *Women Returning to Higher Education*. Buckingham: Open University Press

Perry, W G (1970) *Forms of Intellectual and Ethical Development in the College Years*. New York: Holt, Rinehart and Winston

Price, J (1988) *Motherhood: what it does to your mind*. London: Pandora Press

Pugh, G (1998) Early years training in context. In L Abbott and G Pugh (eds) *Training to Work in the Early Years: developing the climbing frame*. Buckingham: Open University Press

Putnam, R D (2000) *Bowling Alone: the collapse and revival of American community*. New York: Simon and Schuster

QCA (2000) *Curriculum Guidance for the Foundation Stage*. Sudbury: Qualifications and Curriculum Authority

Qizilbash, M (2008) Amartya Sen's capability view: insightful sketch or distorted picture? In F Comim, M Qizilbash and S Alkire (eds) *The Capability Approach: concepts, measures and applications*. Cambridge: Cambridge University Press

Reay, D (1998) Class Work: mothers' involvement in their children's primary schooling. London: UCL Press

Reay, D (2000) A useful extension of Bourdieu's conceptual framework?: emotional capital as a way of understanding mothers' involvement in their children's education? *The Sociological Review* 48(4) p568-85

Richardson, D and Robinson, V (eds) (2008) *Gender and Women's Studies* (3rd ed). Basingstoke: Palgrave Macmillan

Robeyns, I (2008) Sen's capability approach and feminist concerns. In F Comim, M Qizilbash and S Alkire (eds) *The Capability Approach: concepts, measures and applications*. Cambridge: Cambridge University Press

Saito, M (2003) Amartya Sen's capability approach to education: a critical exploration. *Journal of Philosophy of Education* 37(1) p17-33

SCAA (1996) *Nursery Education: desirable outcomes for children's learning on entering compulsory education*. London: School Curriculum Assessment Authority and DfEE

Schaffer, H R (1996) *Social Development*. Oxford: Blackwell

Schuller, T, Preston, J, Hammond, C, Brassett-Grundy, A and Bynner, J (2004) *The Benefits of Learning: the impact of education on health, family life and social capital*. London: RoutledgeFalmer

Sen, A (1985a) *Commodities and Capabilities*. New Delhi: Oxford University Press

Sen, A (1985b) Well-being, agency and freedom: the Dewey Lectures 1984. *The Journal of Philosophy* 82(4) April p169-84

Sen, A (1987) (edited by Geoffrey Hawthorn) *The Standard of Living*. Cambridge: Cambridge University Press

Sen, A (1992) *Inequality Reexamined*. Oxford: Oxford University Press

Sen, A (1993) Capability and well-being. In M Nussbaum and A Sen (eds) *The Quality of Life*. Oxford: Oxford University Press

Sen, A (1995) Gender inequality and theories of justice. In M Nussbaum and J Glover (eds) *Women, Culture, and Development: a study of human capabilities*. Oxford: Oxford University Press

Sen, A (1999) *Development as Freedom*. Oxford: Oxford University Press

Sen, A and Williams, B (eds) (1982) *Utilitarianism and Beyond.* Cambridge: Cambridge University Press, and Paris: Editions de la Maison des Sciences de l'Homme

Silverman, D (2005) *Doing Qualitative Research* (2nd ed). London: Sage

Simon, A, Owen, C, Moss, P, Petrie, P, Cameron, C, Potts, P and Wigfall, V (2007) *Working Together (1), secondary analysis of the Labour Force Survey to map the numbers and characteristics of the occupations working within social care, childcare, nursing and education.* London: Thomas Coram Research Unit, Institute of Education

Skeggs, B (1997) *Formations of Class and Gender: becoming respectable.* London: Sage

Smart, C (2007) *Personal Life.* Cambridge: Polity Press

Stronach, I and MacLure, M (1997) *Educational Research Undone: the postmodern embrace.* Buckingham: Open University Press

Sure Start Unit (2002) *Birth to Three Matters: a framework to support children in their earliest years.* London: DfES

Ten Have, P (1999) *Doing Conversation Analysis: a practical guide.* London: Sage

Unterhalter, E (2003a) Crossing disciplinary boundaries: the potential of Sen's capability approach for sociologists of education. *British Journal of Sociology of Education* 24(5) p665-69

Unterhalter, E (2003b) The capabilities approach and gendered education: an examination of South African complexities. *Theory and Research in Education* 1(1) p197-223

Unterhalter, E (2005) Global inequality, capabilities, social justice: the millenium development goal for gender equality in education. *International Journal of Education and Development* 25(2) p111-22

Vicinus, M (1985) I*ndependent Women: work and community for single women 1850-1920.* London: Virago

Vincent, C (2000) *Including Parents? Education, citizenship and parental agency.* Buckingham: Open University Press

Walby, S (1990) *Theorizing Patriarchy.* Oxford: Basil Blackwell

Walby, S (1997) *Gender Transformations.* London: Routledge

Walby, S (1999) Transformations of the gendered political economy: changes in women's employment in the United Kingdom. *New Political Economy* 4(2) p195-213

Walford, G (ed) (1991) *Doing Educational Research.* London: Routledge.

Walker, M (2005) Amartya Sen's capability approach and education. *Educational Research in Action* 13(1) p103-10

Walker, M (2006a) *Higher Education Pedagogies: a capabilities approach.* Maidenhead: Open University Press

Walker, M (2006b) Towards a capability-based theory of social justice for education policy-making. *Journal of Education Policy* 21(2) March p163-85

Walker, M (2007) Widening participation in higher education: lifelong learning as capability. In D Asplin (ed) *Philosophical Perspectives on Lifelong Learning.* Dordrecht: Springer Press

Walker, M and Unterhalter, E (eds) (2007) *Amartya Sen's Capability Approach and Social Justice in Education.* Basingstoke: Palgrave Macmillan

Wallis, J (ed) (1996) *Liberal Adult Education: the end of an era?* Nottingham: University of Nottingham, Continuing Education Press

Ward, H (2009) Extra pay needed to coax more men into early years, *TES*, 23 January [accessed online]

Watts, M (2006) What is wrong with widening participation in higher education? In J Satterthwaite and E Atkinson (eds) *Discourse, Resistance and Identity Formation.* Stoke on Trent: Trentham Books

Watts, R (2000) Mary Carpenter: educator of the children of 'perishing and dangerous classes'. In M Hilton and P Hirsch (eds) *Practical Visionaries: women, education and social progress 1790-1930.* Harlow: Pearson Education

Williams, B (1987) The standard of living: interests and capabilities. In A Sen (edited by Geoffrey Hawthorn) *The Standard of Living.* Cambridge: Cambridge University Press

Wilkinson, K and Pickett, R (2009) *The Spirit Level.* London: Allen Lane

Wolf, A (2002) *Does Education Matter? Myths about education and economic growth.* London: Penguin

Wolf, A (2009) Know your place. *Adults Learning* 20(5) January p11

Index